Presented To:

Fran

Presented By:

Dan

Date:

May 13, 2001
(Mothers Day)

GOD'S Little Lessons on Life

for
Women

Honor Books
Tulsa, Oklahoma

7th Printing

God's Little Lessons on Life for Women
ISBN 1-56292-634-9
Copyright © 1999 by Honor Books
P.O. Box 55388
Tulsa, OK 74155

Some devotions drawn from original manuscripts prepared by W. B. Freeman Concepts, Inc., Tulsa, Oklahoma. Edited by Kelli James.

Introduction

God's Word, the Bible, has all the answers and encouragement we need to take on life's puzzling questions and challenging situations with confidence. The Bible contains promises that apply to every area of our lives. There are promises dealing with everything from emotions and trials to relationships and finances.

God's Little Lessons on Life for Women gives you easy access to some of your most-needed answers. This conveniently sized book not only provides you with scriptures covering a multitude of topics, but it illustrates those topics with inspiring stories especially for women.

Just as Jesus taught in parables in order to bring divine mysteries to light, the devotional stories in *God's Little Lessons on Life for Women* will help you to grasp the reality of the Scriptures.

The promises of God are for you and your family. He is always ready and willing to bring them to fulfillment in your life. This book is designed to make you aware of His promises, so you can trust in His desire to take care of you.

Table of Contents

GOD's Little Lessons on Life for Women concerning:

Anger

You must understand this, my beloved: let everyone be quick to listen, slow to speak, slow to anger.

James 1:19 NRSV

A soft answer turns away wrath, but a harsh word stirs up anger.

Proverbs 15:1 RSV

Good sense makes a man slow to anger, and it is his glory to overlook an offense.

Proverbs 19:11 RSV

Fathers, do not provoke your children to anger, but bring them up in the discipline and instruction of the Lord.

Ephesians 6:4 NRSV

How to Find a Lost Temper

Once a little girl suddenly became frustrated and screamed at her parents, *"I hate you! I hate you!"*

Her mother, instead of losing her own temper, asked her daughter to put on her coat. Together they walked to a nearby park where a stream had cut a deep valley into the hillside. There the mother told the girl to yell just as she had inside the house.

"I hate you! I hate you!" shouted the girl. *"I hate you! I hate you!"* echoed the valley.

Startled, the girl looked at her mother and whimpered, "Somebody down there doesn't like me."

"Maybe so," the mother replied. "But see what happens when you tell them you love them."

The little girl did so, and this time she heard a voice replying, *"I love you! I love you!"*

Gazing at her mother in wide-eyed surprise, she stammered, "Look! I made a friend down there."

When we're able to deflect our children's anger with calmness, we can "teach them a lesson," all right—a lesson in self-control that will last far longer than any scolding or answering in kind.

As the ancient Roman sage, Seneca, reminds us, *"The greatest cure for anger is delay."*

Anger

Slowness to anger makes for deep understanding;
a quick-tempered person stockpiles stupidity.

Proverbs 14:29 THE MESSAGE

He that is slow to anger is better than the mighty;
and he that ruleth his spirit than he that taketh a city.

Proverbs 16:32 KJV

Be ye angry, and sin not: let not the sun go down
upon your wrath.

Ephesians 4:26 KJV

If it is possible, as much as depends on you, live
peaceably with all men.

Romans 12:18 NKJV

The Fence

There was a little boy with a bad temper. His father gave him a bag of nails and told him that every time he lost his temper, to hammer a nail in the back fence.

The first day the boy had driven 37 nails into the fence. Then it gradually dwindled down. He discovered it was easier to hold his temper than to drive those nails into the fence.

Finally the day came when the boy didn't lose his temper at all. He told his father about it and the father suggested that the boy now pull out one nail for each day that he was able to hold his temper.

The days passed and the young boy was finally able to tell his father that all the nails were gone. The father took his son by the hand and led him to the fence. He said, "You have done well, my son, but look at the holes in the fence. The fence will never be the same. When you say things in anger, they leave a scar just like this one. You can put a knife in a man and draw it out. It won't matter how many times you say I'm sorry, the wound is still there."

Anxiety

Do not be anxious about anything, but in every-thing, by prayer and petition, with thanksgiving, present your requests to God. And the peace of God, which transcends all understanding, will guard your hearts and your minds in Christ Jesus.

Philippians 4:6-7

For I, the Lord your God, hold your right hand; it is I who say to you, "Fear not, I will help you."

Isaiah 41:13 RSV

These things I have spoken unto you, that in me ye might have peace. In the world ye shall have tribulation: but be of good cheer; I have overcome the world.

John 16:33 KJV

Therefore humble yourselves under the mighty hand of God, that He may exalt you in due time, casting all your care upon Him, for He cares for you.

1 Peter 5:6-7 NKJV

Letting Go

To let go doesn't mean to stop caring, it
  means I can't do it for someone else.
To let go is not to cut myself off, it's the
  realization that I don't control another.
To let go is not to enable, but to allow
  learning from natural consequences.
To let go is to admit powerlessness, which
  means the outcome is not in my hands.
To let go is not to try to change or blame
  another, I can only change myself.
To let go is not to care for, but to care about.
To let go is not to fix, but to be supportive.
To let go is not to be protective, it is to
  permit another to face reality.
To let go is not to deny but to accept.
To let go is not to nag, scold, or argue, but
  to search out my own shortcomings
  and correct them.
To let go is not to criticize and regulate
  anyone but to try to become what I
  dream I can be.
To let go is not to regret the past but to
  grow and live for the future.
To let go is to fear less and love more.

                                                    Anonymous

You'll experience a lot less anxiety in life
when you learn to let go.

Anxiety

Cast thy burden upon the LORD, and he shall sustain thee.

Psalm 55:22 KJV

Come to me, all you who are weary and burdened, and I will give you rest.

Matthew 11:28

I will not abandon you as orphans—I will come to you.

John 14:18 NLT

Do you think anyone is going to be able to drive a wedge between us and Christ's love for us? There is no way! Not trouble, not hard times, not hatred, not hunger, not homelessness, not bullying threats, not backstabbing, not even the worst sins listed in Scripture.

Romans 8:35 THE MESSAGE

Looking Up

In her book, *Glorious Intruder*, Joni Eareckson Tada tells about horseback riding with her older sisters when they were all children. She had a hard time keeping up with them because the pony she was riding was half the size of their mounts.

She didn't mind, but took it as a challenge—until they came to the edge of a river. She says, "My sisters on their big horses thought it was fun and exciting to cross the river at the deepest part. They never seemed to notice that my little pony sank quite a bit deeper. . . . It was scary, but I wasn't about to let them know.

"One crossing in particular sticks in my memory. . . . It had rained earlier that week and the river was brown and swollen. As our horses waded out toward midstream, I became transfixed staring at the swirling waters rushing around the legs of my pony. It made me scared and dizzy. I began to lose my balance in the saddle.

"The voice of my sister Jay finally broke through my panic.

"'Look up, Joni! Keep looking up!'" Focusing on her sister, Joni made it safely to the opposite shore.

When we keep our eyes on Jesus, fear and anxiety will slip away, enabling us to make it to the other side.

Assurance

I wipe away your sins because of who I am. And so, I will forget the wrongs you have done.

Isaiah 43:25 CEV

As far as sunrise is from sunset, he has separated us from our sins.

Psalm 103:12 THE MESSAGE

All that the Father gives me will come to me, and whoever comes to me I will never drive away.

John 6:37

Most assuredly, I say to you, he who hears My word and believes in Him who sent Me has everlasting life, and shall not come into judgment, but has passed from death into life.

John 5:24 NKJV

Yes, Even These

Matthew was a tax collector, a hated man among the Jews for helping Rome tighten its occupation. Even so, Jesus loved Matthew, and eventually chose him as one of His disciples.

Peter had a quick temper, his emotions easily triggered by circumstances. During the most critical hours of Jesus' life on earth, he three times denied knowing Jesus. Even so, Jesus loved Peter and empowered him to lead the early church.

Saul wreaked havoc on the church in Jerusalem, leading raids on the homes of Christians and imprisoning the devout. He consented to the death of Stephen and was one of the official witnesses of his execution. He even requested letters of authority to extend the persecution of the church to other cities, including Damascus. Even so, Jesus loved Saul, appeared to him in a light from heaven, and called him to repentance.

No matter what a person may have done— no matter what their character flaws—Jesus loved them. He loved them to the point of dying on their behalf on the Cross. He died for your enemy, the friend or family member who has disappointed or frustrated you. And He died for you.

Assurance

For by grace you have been saved through faith; and this is not of your own doing, it is the gift of God.

Ephesians 2:8 RSV

And I am sure that God, who began the good work within you, will continue his work until it is finally finished on that day when Christ Jesus comes back again.

Philippians 1:6 NLT

I am the good shepherd; I know my sheep and my sheep know me—just as the Father knows me and I know the Father—and I lay down my life for the sheep.

John 10:14-15

God affirms us, making us a sure thing in Christ, putting his Yes within us. By his Spirit he has stamped us with his eternal pledge—a sure beginning of what he is destined to complete.

2 Corinthians 1:21-22
THE MESSAGE

God Is Always Near

In *Love and Duty,* Anne Purcell writes about seeing Major Jim Statler standing with her pastor outside his study after a Sunday service. She knew instantly that he was there with news about her husband, Ben, who was on active duty in Vietnam. Jim had chilling news: "He was on a helicopter that was shot down . . . he's missing in action."

Anne recalls, "Somewhere in the back of my mind, a little candle flame flickered. This tiny flame was the vestige of my faith." Days passed without word. To her, being the wife of an MIA was like being caught in limbo. She found herself able to pray only one thing: "Help me, dear Father." She says, "I hung onto this important truth—that He would help me—and the flickering flame of my candle of faith began to grow." For five years, Anne Purcell clung to the fact that God was near. Little did she know that during those years before she was reunited with her husband, he was whispering to her from a POW cell, "Anne, find solace and strength in the Lord."

God *is* always near. In every circumstance, He's right there beside you saying, "Rest in the assurance of My strength and love."

Children

For this child I prayed, and the LORD has granted me my petition which I asked of Him. Therefore I also have lent him to the LORD; as long as he lives he shall be lent to the LORD.

1 Samuel 1:27-28 NKJV

And all thy children shall be taught of the LORD; and great shall be the peace of thy children.

Isaiah 54:13 KJV

Only take heed, and guard your life diligently, lest you forget the things which your eyes have seen and lest they depart from your [mind and] heart all the days of your life. Teach them to your children, and your children's children.

Deuteronomy 4:9 AMP

Point your kids in the right direction—when they're old they won't be lost.

Proverbs 22:6 THE MESSAGE

The Attitude Diet

Several years ago, a man was asked to give a commencement address. After he had given his speech, he sat on the platform watching the graduates receive their college degrees. Suddenly, the entire audience began applauding for a student who had earned a perfect 4.0 grade point average. During the applause, a faculty member seated next to the speaker leaned over and said to him, "She may be Miss Genius, but her attitude stinks." The speaker later said, "Without even thinking, my hands stopped clapping in mid-air. I couldn't help but think, *How sad.*"

No matter how beautiful, intelligent, talented, or athletic a child may be, there's no substitute for a positive, loving attitude toward others! The foremost architects of that attitude are not a child's teachers or pastor, but the parents.

Be cognizant of the attitudes you "feed" your children every day. They are the diet of your child's mind, just as food is the diet of your child's body. Don't feed your children junk ideas, sour opinions, rotten theology, poisoned feelings, or wilted enthusiasm. Instead, feed your children with the best and most positive ideas, emotional expressions, and thoughtful opinions you have!

Children

Teach us to number our days aright, that we may gain a heart of wisdom.

Psalm 90:12

Do not boast about tomorrow, for you do not know what a day may bring forth.

Proverbs 27:1 NASB

Why waste your money on what really isn't food? Why work hard for something that doesn't satisfy? Listen carefully to me, and you will enjoy the very best foods.

Isaiah 55:2 CEV

It will be like a woman experiencing the pains of labor. When her child is born, her anguish gives place to joy because she has brought a new person into the world. You have sorrow now, but I will see you again; then you will rejoice, and no one can rob you of that joy.

John 16:21-22 NLT

Just Five More Minutes

A man sat on a park bench next to a woman looking out at the playground.

"That's my daughter," she said, pointing to a little girl who was gliding down the slide. Then, looking at her watch, she called to her daughter, "What do you say we go, Samantha?"

Samantha pleaded, "Just five minutes more, Mom. Please? Just five more minutes." The woman nodded and she continued to play to her heart's content.

Minutes later the mother stood and called, "Time to go now." Again the girl pleaded, "Five more minutes, Mom, just five more minutes." Her mother smiled and said, "Okay."

"My, you certainly are a patient mother," the man responded.

"Last year," she said, "our son Tommy was killed by a drunk driver while riding his bike near here. I never spent much time with Tommy and now I'd give anything for just five more minutes with him. I vowed I wouldn't make the same mistake with Samantha. She thinks *she* has five more minutes to swing. Truth is, I get five more minutes with her."

There will be plenty of opportunity for your child to experience disappointment in life, without you being the cause of it. Next time you become impatient with your child, ask yourself: Would you really be in such a rush if this were your child's last day on earth?

Comfort

Blessed be the God and Father of our Lord Jesus Christ, the Father of mercies and God of all comfort, who comforts us in all our affliction so that we will be able to comfort those who are in any affliction with the comfort with which we ourselves are comforted by God.

2 Corinthians 1:3-4 NASB

But the Comforter, which is the Holy Ghost, whom the Father will send in my name, he shall teach you all things, and bring all things to your remembrance, whatsoever I have said unto you.

John 14:26 KJV

The LORD is good, a refuge in times of trouble. He cares for those who trust in him.

Nahum 1:7

Come to me, all who labor and are heavy laden, and I will give you rest.

Matthew 11:28 RSV

Comforting Retreat

Have you ever explored a tidal pool? Low tide is the perfect time to find a myriad of creatures that have temporarily washed ashore from the depths of the sea.

Children are often amazed that they can pick up these shelled creatures and stare at them eyeball to eyeball. The creatures rarely exhibit any form of overt fear, such as moving to attack or attempting to scurry away. The creatures simply withdraw into their shells, instinctively knowing they are safe as long as they remain in their strong, cozy shelters.

Likewise, we are safe when we remain in Christ. We are protected from the hassles of life and the fear of unknowns. Those things will come against us, much like the fingers of a brave and curious child try to invade the sea creature's shell, but they have no power to harm us when we retreat into the shelter of Christ.

The Lord commanded us to learn to *abide* in Him and to *remain* steadfast in our faith. He tells us to *trust* in Him absolutely, and to *shelter* ourselves under His strong wings and in the cleft of His rock-like presence. He delights when we *retreat* into His arms for comfort and tender expressions of love.

Comfort

GOD's a safe-house for the battered, a sanctuary during bad times.

Psalm 9:9 THE MESSAGE

Though I am surrounded by troubles, you will preserve me against the anger of my enemies.

Psalm 138:7 NLT

Wait for the LORD; be strong and take heart and wait for the LORD.

Psalm 27:14

We share in the terrible sufferings of Christ, but also in the wonderful comfort he gives.

2 Corinthians 1:5 CEV

Talk to God

In the midst of her intense grief, Betty found it very difficult to pray. She was drowning in a sea of turbulent emotions and hardly knew her own name, much less what to request from God.

One afternoon, a friend of Betty's came by and soon, Betty was pouring out all of her hurts, fears, and struggles to her. She admitted she was angry with God, and disappointed that her prayers for her husband's healing weren't answered. She admitted she was having difficulty believing God would do anything for her—in the present or the future. Finally, as the well of Betty's emotions began to run dry, her friend said quietly, "I have only one piece of advice to give you. Let's talk to God."

Betty's friend put her arms around her and prayed a simple, heartfelt prayer. After she had finished, she said, "Christ is with you. He is in you. And where He is, because of Who He is, He heals."

No matter what you may be going through today, your best recourse is to invite Jesus Christ to manifest Himself in you and through you. He gives you Himself, and in Him is all the power, strength, encouragement, love, and comfort you need.

Commitment

As you therefore have received Christ Jesus the Lord, so walk in Him, rooted and built up in Him and established in the faith, as you have been taught, abounding in it with thanksgiving.

Colossians 2:6-7 NKJV

With all these things in mind, dear brothers and sisters, stand firm and keep a strong grip on everything we taught you both in person and by letter.

2 Thessalonians 2:15 NLT

Commit your way to the LORD; trust in him and he will do this: He will make your righteousness shine like the dawn, the justice of your cause like the noonday sun.

Psalm 37:5-6

So if you find life difficult because you're doing what God said, take it in stride. Trust him. He knows what he's doing, and he'll keep on doing it.

1 Peter 4:19 THE MESSAGE

Commit to Hope

Anita Septimus has worked as a social worker for HIV-infected children since 1985. In the first few months she worked with her tiny clients, three of them died. Despair began to overwhelm her. She made a commitment to stick with the job for three more months, during which time she could not get a friend's words out of her thoughts, "You have not chosen a pretty profession."

She had to admit her friend was right. It took resolve to accept that fact and simply do what she could to help families make the most of what remained of their children's lives. She is still there.

Over the last ten years, her clinic has grown considerably. Today, Anita and her staff care for more than 300 families with AIDS children. They go into their homes, teach infection prevention, and help parents plan for the future.

One AIDS baby wasn't expected to see her first birthday, but she recently celebrated her tenth. Such "long-term" clients give back to Anita what she terms "an indestructible sense of hope"—a precious gift!

When you make a commitment to sow hope into the lives of others, you will reap back tremendous hope for your own life.

Commitment

Let your heart therefore be loyal to the LORD our God, to walk in His statutes and keep His commandments, as at this day.

1 Kings 8:61 NKJV

Commit your work to the LORD, and then your plans will succeed.

Proverbs 16:3 NLT

Now all has been heard; here is the conclusion of the matter: Fear God and keep his commandments, for this is the whole duty of man.

Ecclesiastes 12:13

Turn your back on evil, work for the good and don't quit. GOD loves this kind of thing, never turns away from his friends.

Psalm 37:27 THE MESSAGE

Hull House

Jane was only seven years old when she visited a shabby street in a nearby town, and seeing ragged children there, announced that she wanted to build a big house so poor children would have a place to play. As a young adult, Jane and a friend visited Toynbee Hall in London, where they saw educated people helping the poor by living among them.

She and her friend returned to Chicago, restored an old mansion, and moved in! There they cared for children of working mothers and held sewing and cooking classes. Older boys and girls had clubs at the mansion. An art gallery and public music, reading, and craft rooms were created in the mansion. Her dream came true!

Jane didn't stop there. She spoke up for people who couldn't speak for themselves. She was eventually awarded an honorary degree from Yale. President Theodore Roosevelt dubbed her "America's most useful citizen," and she was awarded the Nobel Prize for Peace.

No matter how famous she became, however, Jane Addams remained a resident of Hull House. She died there, in the heart of the slum she had come to call home.

When we commit our dreams and plans to the Lord, He will see to it that they come to pass.

Confidence

So we are always confident, knowing that while we are at home in the body we are absent from the Lord. For we walk by faith, not by sight.

2 Corinthians 5:6-7 NKJV

Let us then approach the throne of grace with confidence, so that we may receive mercy and find grace to help us in our time of need.

Hebrews 4:16

We have confidence to enter the holy place by the blood of Jesus.

Hebrews 10:19 NASB

For the Lord shall be your confidence, firm and strong, and shall keep your foot from being caught [in a trap or hidden danger].

Proverbs 3:26 AMP

Always Useful to God

In *Glorious Intruder*, Joni Eareckson Tada writes about Diane, who suffers from multiple sclerosis: "In her quiet sanctuary, Diane turns her head slightly on the pillow toward the corkboard on the wall. Her eyes scan each thumbtacked card and list. Each photo. Every torn piece of paper carefully pinned in a row. The stillness is broken as Diane begins to murmur. She is praying.

"Some would look at Diane—stiff and motionless—and shake their heads . . . 'What a shame. Her life has no meaning. She can't really do anything.' But Diane is confident, convinced her life is significant. Her labor of prayer counts. She pushes back the kingdom of darkness that blackens the alleys and streets of east Los Angeles. She aids homeless mothers, single parents, abused children, despondent teenagers, handicapped boys, and dying and forgotten old people. Diane is on the front lines, advancing the gospel of Christ, holding up weak saints, inspiring doubting believers, energizing other prayer warriors, and delighting her Lord and Savior."

What a difference we can make, regardless of our situation in life, if we have confidence in God's desire to use us. God is willing and able to use us regardless of our ability or inability—He always has a plan!

Confidence

Remember the word that I said to you, "A servant is not greater than his master." If they persecuted Me, they will also persecute you.

John 15:20 NKJV

Blessed are those who have been persecuted for the sake of righteousness, for theirs is the kingdom of heaven.

Matthew 5:10 NASB

Everyone who wants to live a godly life in Christ Jesus will suffer persecution.

2 Timothy 3:12 NLT

We are hard pressed on every side, but not crushed; perplexed, but not in despair; persecuted, but not abandoned; struck down, but not destroyed.

2 Corinthians 4:8-9

He's Holding You

Many years ago, a young woman who felt called into the ministry was accepted into a well-known seminary. There were only two other women enrolled there, and her very presence seemed to make her male classmates uncomfortable. She felt isolated. To make matters worse, many of her professors were doing their best to destroy her faith rather than build it up. Even her private devotions seemed dry and lonely.

At Christmas break she sought her father's counsel. "How can I be strong in my resolve and straight in my theology with all that I face there?"

Her father took a pencil from his pocket and laid it on the palm of his hand. "Can that pencil stand upright by itself?" he asked her.

"No," she replied. Then her father grasped the pencil in his hand and held it in an upright position. "Ah," she said, "but you are holding it now."

"Daughter," he replied, "your life is like this pencil. But Jesus Christ is the One who can hold you." The young woman took her father's pencil and returned to seminary.

Whatever difficulties you may confront today, you can be confident that it is God who holds you in His hands. His strength holds you up and enables you to face anything that comes your way.

Contentment

To everyone who is thirsty, he gives something to drink; to everyone who is hungry, he gives good things to eat.

Psalm 107:9 CEV

Better is a little with righteousness than great revenues without right.

Proverbs 16:8 KJV

Better is an handful with quietness, than both the hands full with travail and vexation of spirit.

Ecclesiastes 4:6 KJV

Not that I complain of want; for I have learned, in whatever state I am, to be content.

Philippians 4:11 RSV

Eight Requirements for Contented Living

Health enough to make work a pleasure.
Wealth enough to support your needs.
Strength enough to battle with
        difficulties and overcome them.
Grace enough to confess your sins and put
        them behind you.
Patience enough to toil until some good
        is accomplished.
Faith enough to make real the things of God.
Hope enough to remove all anxious fear
        about the future.
Charity enough to see some good in everyone.

Johann Wolfgang von Goethe

Contentment

Now godliness with contentment is great gain.
1 Timothy 6:6 NKJV

Let your conversation be without covetousness;
and be content with such things as ye have: for he
hath said, I will never leave thee, nor forsake thee.
Hebrews 13:5 KJV

That's why we can be so sure that every detail in our
lives of love for God is worked into something good.
Romans 8:28 THE MESSAGE

It is not that we think we can do anything of
lasting value by ourselves. Our only power and
success come from God.
2 Corinthians 3:5 NLT

Contentment Is . . .

In her book, *Startled by Silence,* Ruth Senter tells the following story of what contentment means:

"I heard the voice, but I couldn't see the person.

"'Delores, I really appreciated the book you picked up for me. . . . I haven't been able to put the book down.'

"For a moment, the melodious voice was silent, then I heard it again.

"'Have you ever seen such a gorgeous day?'

"The voice was too good to be true. Who can be thankful at this time of morning? Probably some rich woman who has nothing to do all day but sip tea and read.

"I rounded the corner and came face to face with the youthful voice. Her yellow housekeeping uniform hung crisp and neat on her fiftyish frame— she was an employee of the facility at which I swam.

"I still had the yellow uniform on my mind as I sank down into the whirlpool. My two companions were deep in conversation.

"'The water is too hot, the whirlpool jets aren't strong enough . . . ' With a diamond-studded hand, one of them wiped the white suds out of his face.

"The yellow uniform and the diamond-studded ring stood out in striking, silent contrast, proof to me again that when God says, 'Godliness with contentment is great gain,' He really means it."

Courage

Be of good courage, and he shall strengthen your heart, all ye that hope in the LORD.

Psalm 31:24 KJV

Be strong and courageous, do not fear or be dismayed . . . for the one with us is greater than the one with him.

2 Chronicles 32:7 NASB

Yes, be bold and strong! Banish fear and doubt! For remember, the Lord your God is with you wherever you go.

Joshua 1:9 TLB

Wait patiently for the LORD. Be brave and courageous. Yes, wait patiently for the LORD.

Psalm 27:14 NLT

The Paraclete

A man who was about to undergo open heart surgery was visited in his room by a nurse. She took hold of his hand. She told him that during his surgery the next day he would be disconnected from his heart and kept alive by certain machines. Then once his heart was restored and the operation was over he would eventually wake up in a special recovery room.

"You may be immobile for as long as six hours," she said. "You may be unable to move, or speak, or even to open your eyes, but you will be perfectly conscious and you will hear and you will know everything that is going on around you. During those six hours I will be at your side and I will hold your hand, exactly as I am doing now. I will stay with you until you are fully recovered. Although you may feel absolutely helpless, when you feel my hand, you will know that I will not leave you."

Jesus sent the Holy Spirit to walk alongside us and hold our hand. He is the "paraclete," the One called alongside. Whatever you face you can take courage, knowing that He is always with you.

Courage

And so we should not be like cringing, fearful slaves, but we should behave like God's very own children, adopted into the bosom of his family, and calling to him, "Father, Father."

Romans 8:15 TLB

Light, space, zest—that's GOD! So, with him on my side I'm fearless, afraid of no one and nothing.

Psalm 27:1 THE MESSAGE

For I am the LORD, your God, who takes hold of your right hand and says to you, Do not fear; I will help you.

Isaiah 41:13

Overwhelming victory is ours through Christ who loved us enough to die for us.

Romans 8:37 TLB

Eyes on the Goal

A television drama called "See How She Runs," tells the story of a forty-year-old divorcee who decided to become a jogger. She eventually entered the Boston Marathon.

As she ran, huge blisters developed on her feet. She was also hit and injured by a bicycle. And several miles short of the finish line, she was utterly exhausted. Yet she kept going.

Then, within a few hundred yards of the finish line, late at night when most other runners had either finished or dropped out, she fell and lay flat on her face, too tired to raise her head. But her friends had put up a makeshift tape across the finish line and began to cheer her on. She lifted her head, saw the tape, and realized her goal was within sight. She got up on her bruised and bleeding feet, and in a burst of energy dredged up from deep inside her courageous heart, she ran the last few yards.

She had kept her eyes on the goal and for the joy of finishing, she endured.

That's what Jesus did for us. He kept His eyes on the goal and didn't quit. With His strength, we can have the courage to meet whatever challenges lie ahead each and every day.

Death

Yea, though I walk through the valley of the shadow of death, I will fear no evil: for thou art with me; thy rod and thy staff they comfort me.

Psalm 23:4 KJV

Set me as a seal upon your heart, as a seal upon your arm; for love is strong as death, jealousy is cruel as the grave. Its flashes are flashes of fire, a most vehement flame.

Song of Solomon 8:6 RSV

I tell you the truth, if anyone keeps my word, he will never see death.

John 8:51

I heard a loud voice shout from the throne: God's home is now with his people. He will live with them, and they will be his own. Yes, God will make his home among his people. He will wipe all tears from their eyes, and there will be no more death, suffering, crying, or pain. These things of the past are gone forever.

Revelation 21:3-4 CEV

Healing Grief's Wounds

Over recent months, a young girl had gradually begun to understand that she'd never get to play like other girls. And lately, she'd begun to bring up the subject of death.

One day, the little girl asked, "Mama, what is it like to die? Does it hurt?"

Quick tears flooded the mother's eyes. She took a deep breath, and uttered a brief prayer for wisdom.

"Peg," she said, "do you remember when you used to play so hard that when night came you were too tired to undress, and you'd tumble into my bed and fall asleep? Next morning, you'd wake up and find yourself in your own bed, because someone loved you and took care of you?

"Darling," she said softly, "death is something like that. Some day we all wake up to find ourselves in another room—a room where we belong, with the Lord who loves us."

The girl smiled and soon fell asleep in her arms. Not many weeks later she fell asleep just as her mother had said, trusting that her Father in heaven would take her to her new room.

Death may be a difficult subject to discuss with our children, but we must teach them that they have no reason to fear death, that God will always hold them in His loving arms.

Death

Whoever believes in Him should not perish but have eternal life.

John 3:15 NKJV

I will ransom them from the power of the grave; I will redeem them from death.

Hosea 13:14 KJV

He will swallow up death forever! The Sovereign LORD will wipe away all tears.

Isaiah 25:8 NLT

For to me, to live is Christ and to die is gain.

Philippians 1:21

The Shadow of Death

For those left in grief when a loved one dies, the pain of the loss can be soothed by the assurance that those who have put their faith in the Lord have nothing to fear in death. The truth of this was brought home through a very simple analogy used by a well-known preacher.

"Dr. Donald Grey Barnhouse was one of America's great preachers. His first wife died from cancer when she was in her thirties, leaving three children under the age of twelve. Barnhouse chose to preach the funeral sermon himself. What does a father tell his motherless children at a time like that?

"On the way to the service, he was driving with his little family when a large truck passed them on the highway, casting a shadow over their car. Barnhouse turned to his oldest daughter who was staring disconsolately out the windows, and asked, 'Tell me, sweetheart, would you rather be run over by that truck or its shadow?'

"The little girl looked curiously at her father and said, 'by the shadow, I guess. It can't hurt you.'

"Dr. Barnhouse said quietly to the three children, 'Your mother has not been overrun by death, but by the shadow of death. That is nothing to fear.'"

Encouragement

The righteous face many troubles, but the LORD
rescues them from each and every one.

Psalm 34:19 NLT

The Lord says, "If you love me and truly know
who I am, I will rescue you and keep you safe.
When you are in trouble, call out to me. I will
answer and be there to protect and honor you."

Psalm 91:14-15 CEV

These things I have spoken unto you, that in me
ye might have peace. In the world ye shall have
tribulation: but be of good cheer; I have overcome
the world.

John 16:33 KJV

Humble yourselves therefore under the mighty hand
of God, that in due time he may exalt you. Cast all
your anxieties on him, for he cares about you.

1 Peter 5:6-7 RSV

The Flint That Lights
Other People's Torches

Author Phyllis Theroux writes about how her father helped her deal with failure:

"If there was any one thing my father did for me when I was growing up it was to give me the promise that ahead of me was dry land—a bright, marshless territory, without chuckholes or traps, where one day I would walk easily and as befitting my talents. . . .

"Thus it was, when he came upon me one afternoon sobbing out my unsuccesses into a wet pillow, that he sat down on the bed and assured me that my grief was only a temporary setback. Oh, very temporary! Why, he couldn't think of any other little girl who was so talented, so predestined to succeed in every department as I was. 'And don't forget,' he added with a smile, 'that we can trace our ancestry right back to Pepin the Stupid!'

"There are some people who carry the flint that lights other people's torches. . . . That was my father's gift to me."

Today before the sun goes down, your child is likely to experience one of those "unsuccesses" that need your simple comforting words, "this, too, shall pass." Be watchful for the opportunity to give your child this unforgettable, invaluable experience.

Encouragement

God's love, though, is ever and always, eternally present to all who fear him, making everything right for them and their children as they follow his Covenant ways and remember to do whatever he said.

Psalm 103:17-18
THE MESSAGE

Trust in the Lord instead. Be kind and good to others; then you will live safely here in the land and prosper, feeding in safety. Be delighted with the Lord. Then he will give you all your heart's desires.

Psalm 37:3-4 TLB

The humble will see their God at work and be glad. Let all who seek God's help live in joy.

Psalm 69:32 NLT

But exhort one another daily, while it is called "Today," lest any of you be hardened through the deceitfulness of sin.

Hebrews 3:13 NKJV

At the Counter

Paula was in the airport, on her way home from Easter vacation. It had been miserable. Her heart was heavy at the devastation in her daughter's life. Her husband of one year had left her and she was immobilized by shock and sorrow.

As Paula stopped to buy souvenirs for her grandchildren, the clerk asked her how she liked her home state.

"It's beautiful," Paula replied.

"What did you see on your vacation?" the clerk asked.

Paula's eyes filled with tears. "It wasn't a vacation. Just a serious family problem. My daughter is going through a very difficult time and I hate to leave her."

"Oh, but God is good. He will work on your daughter's behalf."

"I know," whispered Paula through her tears. And she left with more than just her small purchase. She took away a touch of Christ's resurrection power—the power of God's love to reach out and touch a hurting heart.

The Bible tells us that "He who waters will himself be watered." (See Proverbs 11:25.) When we are ready and available to give a word of encouragement to someone in need, God will see to it that we receive that touch of His love when we need it most.

Failure

If the LORD delights in a man's way, he makes his steps firm; though he stumble, he will not fall, for the LORD upholds him with his hand.

Psalm 37:23-24

For whatever is born of God overcomes the world. And this is the victory that has overcome the world— our faith.

1 John 5:4 NKJV

The steadfast love of the Lord never ceases, his mercies never come to an end; they are new every morning; great is thy faithfulness.

Lamentations 3:22 RSV

Give us help for the hard task; human help is worthless. In God we'll do our very best; he'll flatten the opposition for good.

Psalm 60:12 THE MESSAGE

Starting Over

In 1991, Anne Busquet was General Manager of the Optima card division for American Express. When five of her 2,000 employees were found to have hidden $24 million in losses, she was held accountable. Busquet had to face the fact that, because she was an intense perfectionist, she apparently came across as intimidating and confrontational to her subordinates—so much so, they were more willing to lie than to report bad news to her!

Busquet lost her Optima job but was given a second chance by American Express: An opportunity to salvage one of its smaller businesses. Her self-esteem shaken, she nearly turned down the offer. However, she decided this was her chance to improve the way she related to others. She took on the new job as a personal challenge to change.

Realizing she had to be much more understanding, she began to work on being more patient and listening more carefully and intently. She learned to solicit bad news in a reassuring way.

Four years after she was removed from her previous position, Anne Busquet was promoted to an executive vice-president position at American Express.

Failure is not the end; it is a teacher for a new beginning and a better life!

Failure

If God is for us, who can be against us? He who did not spare his own Son, but gave him up for us all—how will he not also, along with him, graciously give us all things?

Romans 8:31-32

Now thanks be to God who always leads us in triumph in Christ, and through us diffuses the fragrance of His knowledge in every place.

2 Corinthians 2:14 NKJV

All of us have sinned and fallen short of God's glory. But God treats us much better than we deserve, and because of Christ Jesus, he freely accepts us and sets us free from our sins.

Romans 3:23-24 CEV

God-loyal people don't stay down long; soon they're up on their feet, while the wicked end up flat on their faces.

Proverbs 24:16 THE MESSAGE

Giving God All

Janette Oke, a best-selling novelist with more than forty books to her credit, is considered the modern-day "pioneer author" for Christian fiction. When she first decided to write, she said to God, "Lord, I'm going to write this book. If it works, and if I discover I have talent, I'll give it all to You."

Janette sensed God was not pleased with the bargain she was trying to strike with Him. She felt in her heart as if He was responding, "If you're serious about this, then I want everything before you start." Thus she gave Him her ambitions and dreams, and trusted Him with the outcome of her efforts. She left it up to Him to teach her, whether she was successful or not. And a shelf of novels later, Janette Oke has proven "God can teach spiritual truths through fictional characters."

The greatest step of faith is to trust God *before* we see the results of our efforts. Whether we fail or succeed, God will still be with us. God doesn't ask for our best, He asks us for our selves. When we give Him everything He can use even our failures to bring us to eventual success.

Faith

So now, since we have been made right in God's sight by faith in his promises, we can have real peace with him because of what Jesus Christ our Lord has done for us. For because of our faith, he has brought us into this place of highest privilege where we now stand, and we confidently and joyfully look forward to actually becoming all that God has had in mind for us to be.

Romans 5:1-2 TLB

They are justified by his grace as a gift, through the redemption which is in Christ Jesus, whom God put forward as an expiation by his blood, to be received by faith. This was to show God's righteousness, because in his divine forbearance he had passed over former sins.

Romans 3:24-25 RSV

But without faith it is impossible to please him: for he that cometh to God must believe that he is, and that he is a rewarder of them that diligently seek him.

Hebrews 11:6 KJV

For ye are all the children of God by faith in Christ Jesus.

Galatians 3:26 KJV

A Tug on the Line

A twelve-year-old girl accepted Jesus Christ as her personal Savior and Lord during a weekend revival meeting. The next week, her school friends questioned her about the experience.

"Did you hear God talk?" one asked.

"No," the girl said.

"Did you have a vision?" another asked.

"No," the girl replied.

"Well, how did you know it was God?" a third friend asked.

The girl thought for a moment and then said, "It's like when you catch a fish. You can't see the fish or hear the fish; you just feel him tugging on your line. I felt God tugging on my heart."

So often we try to figure out life by what we can see, hear, or experience with our other senses. We make calculated estimates and judgments based on empirical evidence. There's a level of truth, however, that cannot be perceived by the senses or measured objectively. It's at that level where faith abounds. It is our faith that compels us to believe, even when we cannot explain to others why or how. By our faith, we only know in Whom we trust. And that is sufficient.

Faith

What is faith? It is the confident assurance that something we want is going to happen. It is the certainty that what we hope for is waiting for us, even though we cannot see it up ahead.

Hebrews 11:1 TLB

We live by faith, not by sight.

2 Corinthians 5:7

If you can believe, all things are possible to him who believes.

Mark 9:23 NKJV

And now just as you trusted Christ to save you, trust him, too, for each day's problems; live in vital union with him.

Colossians 2:6 TLB

Blind Faith

Dr. Amanda Whitworth was frustrated as she crept up a hill with eight cars in front of her. They were stuck behind a slow-moving truck, and she was in a hurry. Amanda's last patient had needed more attention than was allotted for regular examinations, and she was late leaving to pick up her daughter from day school. Now she breathed a prayer that she would not be late again. It would be her third time, and because the day school did not tolerate parental tardiness, she would have to make new arrangements for Allie's afternoon care.

Amanda silently fumed at the truck's progress. No one dared pass the truck, as it was impossible to see oncoming cars around it. Suddenly, the truck driver waved his hand indicating that all was clear ahead. As Amanda zipped past him, it occurred to her that this man was probably a stranger to all who passed him—yet nine people trusted their lives to this man.

What a tremendous picture of how we do all that we can do, and then we must trust even the smallest details of our lives to the care of God, our loving Heavenly Father. It's comforting to know that He can always see exactly what's ahead!

Family

A man must leave his father and mother when he marries, so that he can be perfectly joined to his wife, and the two shall be one.

Ephesians 5:31 TLB

Children, obey your parents in the Lord, for this is right. Honor your father and mother (which is the first commandment with a promise), so that it may be well with you, and that you may live long on the earth.

Ephesians 6:1-3 NASB

Be very careful never to forget what you have seen God doing for you. May his miracles have a deep and permanent effect upon your lives! Tell your children and your grandchildren about the glorious miracles he did.

Deuteronomy 4:9 TLB

But if anyone does not provide for his own, and especially for those of his household, he has denied the faith, and is worse than an unbeliever.

1 Timothy 5:8 NASB

Raised in Love

"The family," says Mother Teresa, "is the place to learn Jesus. God has sent the family—together as husband and wife and children—to be His love."

In *Words to Love By,* Mother Teresa writes, "Once a lady came to me in great sorrow and told me that her daughter had lost her husband and a child. All the daughter's hatred had turned on the mother.

"So I said, 'Now you think a bit about the little things that your daughter liked when she was a child. Maybe flowers or a special food. Try to give her some of these things without looking for a return.'

"And she started doing some of these things, like putting the daughter's favorite flower on the table, or leaving a beautiful piece of cloth for her. And she did not look for a return from the daughter.

"Several days later the daughter said, 'Mommy, come. I love you. I want you.'

"By being reminded of the joy of childhood, the daughter reconnected with her family. She must have had a happy childhood to go back to the joy and happiness of her mother's love."

Today, think of some special ways to remind your family of your love for them; then put them into action!

Family

And the son said unto him, Father, I have sinned against heaven, and in thy sight, and am no more worthy to be called thy son. But the father said to his servants, Bring forth the best robe, and put it on him; and put a ring on his hand, and shoes on his feet.

Luke 15:21-22 KJV

Even when we were God's enemies, he made peace with us, because his Son died for us. Yet something even greater than friendship is ours. Now that we are at peace with God, we will be saved by his Son's life.

Romans 5:10 CEV

All this is from God, who reconciled us to himself through Christ and gave us the ministry of reconciliation: that God was reconciling the world to himself in Christ, not counting men's sins against them. And he has committed to us the message of reconciliation.

2 Corinthians 5:18-19

You must make allowance for each other's faults and forgive the person who offends you. Remember, the Lord forgave you, so you must forgive others.

Colossians 3:13 NLT

Never Too Late

A successful, respected couple gave their son the best of everything—the best schools, a new sports car, even a management-track position in their company. Then one day, the son was arrested for embezzling funds from their firm.

All through his trial, the young man appeared proud, nonchalant, and unrepentant. Then the jury brought in the verdict: Guilty on all counts. The judge ordered him to stand. He arose, still somewhat cocky and indifferent. As he glanced around the courtroom, he noticed that his parents too were standing. The young man stared at them for a long time. He began to realize that this couple, who once strode so confidently with their heads high and straight, now stood with their backs stooped, their heads bowed with sorrow.

His parents were acknowledging that they were partly responsible for what the son had become. They were prepared to receive, as though it was for themselves, their son's sentence from the judge.

At the sight of his parents, bent and humiliated, the son began to weep bitterly, and for the first time showed remorse for his crime.

Although our children are ultimately responsible for their own behavior as adults, we are responsible to train them to make the right choices in life.

Favor

Never let loyalty and kindness get away from you!
Wear them like a necklace; write them deep within
your heart. Then you will find favor with both God
and people, and you will gain a good reputation.

Proverbs 3:3-4 NLT

And Jesus grew in wisdom and stature, and in favor
with God and men.

Luke 2:52

But God was with him and delivered him out of
all his troubles, and gave him favor and wisdom in
the presence of Pharaoh, king of Egypt; and he
made him governor over Egypt; and all his house.

Acts 7:9-10 NKJV

Fools don't care if they are wrong, but God is
pleased when people do right.

Proverbs 14:9 CEV

The Favor of God

The story is told of a king who owned a valuable diamond, one of the rarest and most perfect in the world. One day the diamond fell and a deep scratch marred its face. The king summoned the best diamond experts in the land to correct the blemish, but they all agreed they could not remove the scratch without cutting away a good part of the surface, thus reducing the weight and value of the diamond.

Finally one expert appeared and assured him that he could fix the diamond without reducing its value. His confidence was convincing and the king gave the diamond to the man. In a few days, the artisan returned the diamond to the king, who was amazed to find that the ugly scratch was gone, and in its place a beautiful rose was etched. The former scratch had become the stem of an exquisite flower!

Any mistake we make in life may temporarily mar our reputation. But if we stick to what we know is right and continue to attempt to conform our will to that of God, we can trust Him to turn the "scratches" on our souls into part of His signature—that's what it means to have God's favor.

Favor

For surely, O LORD, you bless the righteous; you surround them with your favor as with a shield.

Psalm 5:12

A good name is to be chosen rather than great riches, loving favor rather than silver and gold.

Proverbs 22:1 NKJV

They did not conquer by their own strength and skill, but by your mighty power and because you smiled upon them and favored them.

Psalm 44:3 TLB

For whoever finds me finds life and wins approval from the LORD.

Proverbs 8:35 NLT

Favor for a Lifetime

The Psalms tell us that God's favor is for a lifetime. Wherever we go in life, whatever circumstances we face, God looks upon us with His favor and desires to show us His lovingkindness.

In *Unto the Hills,* Billy Graham reminds us of the story of God's favor toward Joseph. He says, "Joseph would never have been of use to God had he not been sold into slavery by brothers who hated him and wrongly accused by Potiphar, who put in him prison. Even after he had told Pharaoh's cupbearer he would be restored to the king's court and asked him to tell Pharaoh of his unjust imprisonment, Joseph had to wait two more years for release from prison.

"All of this was God's preparation for Joseph's ultimate rise to a position of power and authority second only to that of Pharaoh himself, a position he used to feed all of Israel during a famine.

"As we wait upon the Lord, God may sometimes seem slow in coming to help us, but He never comes too late. His timing is always perfect. How could it not be so from a God who favors us, as we do our children, for a lifetime?"

Fear

Fear thou not; for I am with thee: be not dismayed; for I am thy God: I will strengthen thee; yea, I will help thee; yea, I will uphold thee with the right hand of my righteousness.

Isaiah 41:10 KJV

God's Spirit doesn't make cowards out of us. The Spirit gives us power, love, and self-control.

2 Timothy 1:7 CEV

Peace I leave with you; my peace I give you. I do not give to you as the world gives. Do not let your hearts be troubled and do not be afraid.

John 14:27

But when I am afraid, I put my trust in you. O God, I praise your word. I trust in God, so why should I be afraid? What can mere mortals do to me?

Psalm 56:3-4 NLT

Overcoming Fear

When Beth's boss asked her to take on an extra project, Beth saw the opportunity to prove she could handle greater responsibility. She immediately began to think how she might approach the task and her enthusiasm ran high. But when the time came to start the project, Beth found herself telling her boss she was too busy to do it justice. The project was given to someone else, who earned a promotion for completing it successfully. Beth didn't receive any new opportunities and eventually took a position with another firm.

What had kept Beth from doing the project? Simple procrastination. She put off getting started on the job until she was paralyzed with fear—fear that she might not be able to do the job or that her performance would not meet her boss's expectations. In the end, Beth didn't move ahead and thus reinforced her fears with a bigger sense of insecurity about her own ability.

If you find yourself procrastinating, ask God to show you how to overcome your fear, then do what He says. He wants you to succeed and live a fulfilled life, but you must step out in faith—He's waiting to bless you!

Fear

But from everlasting to everlasting the LORD's love is with those who fear him, and his righteousness with their children's children—with those who keep his covenant and remember to obey his precepts.

Psalm 103:17-18

In the day when I cried thou answeredst me, and strengthenedst me with strength in my soul. Though I walk in the midst of trouble, thou wilt revive me.

Psalm 138:3,7 KJV

Be strong and of good courage, do not fear nor be afraid of them; for the LORD your God, He is the One who goes with you. He will not leave you nor forsake you.

Deuteronomy 31:6 NKJV

Trust in the Lord instead. Be kind and good to others; then you will live safely here in the land and prosper, feeding in safety. Be delighted with the Lord. Then he will give you all your heart's desires.

Psalm 37:3-4 TLB

Face Your Fear

In 1993, a deranged fan stabbed tennis star Monica Seles, narrowly missing her spinal cord. She recognized her assailant as a man she had seen loitering around her hotel, but she had no idea why he had attacked her. At the hospital, she couldn't stop asking, *What if he comes back?* That night, her parents and brother all stayed in her hospital room with her. Monica was assured that her attacker was in custody. Even so, she had flashbacks of his face, the blood-stained knife, and her own screams.

Six months after the attack, her assailant was given two years' probation and set free. Her fear intensified, and she sought out a psychologist to help her. Encouraged by her peers, she made a decision to return to tennis. Then came yet another blow. A German judge upheld her assailant's suspended sentence, which had been appealed. She said to herself, *Monica, you have to move on.* Three months later, she played an exhibition match and scored two wins—one on the court, and one in her mind and heart.

Are you facing an obstacle that seems insurmountable? Be encouraged. The God Who never leaves you or forsakes you will be with you, strengthening you every step of the way.

Forgiveness

If you forgive those who sin against you, your heavenly Father will forgive you.

Matthew 6:14 NLT

Whenever you stand praying, forgive, if you have anything against anyone, so that your Father who is in heaven will also forgive you your transgressions.

Mark 11:25-26 NASB

But love your enemies, do good, and lend, hoping for nothing in return.

Luke 6:35 NKJV

Forbearing one another and, if one has a complaint against another, forgiving each other; as the Lord has forgiven you, so you also must forgive.

Colossians 3:13 RSV

Broken Silence

Meredith was surprised to find a letter in the mailbox from her brother, Tim. It had been three years since she had spoken to him, even though they lived in the same town. In the letter, Tim told her he and his wife were expecting twins and he hoped she would come to visit the babies after they were born. He expressed his sorrow that they had not communicated more, and apologized for whatever it was he had done to cause them to become estranged.

Meredith's initial reaction was one of anger. "Whatever it was?" Didn't he know? She immediately sat down and wrote a five-page letter detailing all the things Tim had done to hurt her. When she read her letter, however, she was horrified by what she found.

She had thought she was being very matter-of-fact, but her words were full of anger and pain. Tears of forgiveness filled her eyes. Perhaps it wasn't all Tim's fault.

You may not even realize you're harboring past hurts until something comes along to expose your pain. But when you forgive and release your hurts into God's hands, He can cleanse your heart and mind with His love and forgiveness and give you the power to forgive.

Forgiveness

You are forgiving and good, O Lord, abounding
in love to all who call to you.
Psalm 86:5

Come now, let us reason together, says the LORD:
though your sins are like scarlet, they shall be as
white as snow; though they are red like crimson,
they shall become like wool.
Isaiah 1:18 RSV

Our God, no one is like you. We are all that is left
of your chosen people, and you freely forgive our
sin and guilt. You don't stay angry forever; you're
glad to have pity.
Micah 7:18 CEV

Dear friends, if a Christian is overcome by some
sin, you who are godly should gently and humbly
help that person back onto the right path. And be
careful not to fall into the same temptation yourself.
Galatians 6:1 NLT

Fishing for Sins

A young girl and her mother were returning home from a shopping mall, and the girl had acted badly—running off, being uncooperative, wanting this and that, etc. She could tell her mother was in a bad mood, and she tried to broach the subject of her behavior.

"When we ask God to forgive us when we are bad," she asked, "He does, doesn't He?"

"Yes, He does," her mother replied.

"And when He forgives us He doesn't remember them anymore, right?" the daughter asked.

"That's right," said her mother, growing more charitable. "It's like the song we sing at church, that God buries our sins in the deepest sea."

The girl was silent for awhile. Then she said, "I've asked God to forgive me, and now I want to ask you to promise me something."

"What's that?" said her mother, pleased at this display of contrition.

"I want you to promise that when we get home you won't go fishing for those sins, okay?"

Most mothers can identify with the impression this child has received from her mother. One of the most important lessons we can teach by example is that forgiven sins stay forgiven—no fishing allowed.

Friendship

Share each other's troubles and problems, and in this way obey the law of Christ.

Galatians 6:2 NLT

Whoever loves his brother [believer] abides (lives) in the Light, and in It or in him there is no occasion for stumbling or cause for error or sin.

1 John 2:10 AMP

Your friend, and your father's friend, do not forsake.

Proverbs 27:10 RSV

Greater love has no one than this, than to lay down one's life for his friends.

John 15:13 NKJV

Love Believes the Best

One of the noblest friendships in literature is that of Melanie and Scarlett in Margaret Mitchell's classic, *Gone with the Wind*. Melanie is characterized as a woman who "always saw the best in everyone and remarked kindly upon it." Even when Scarlett tries to confess her shameful behavior toward Melanie's husband Ashley, Melanie says, "Darling, I don't want any explanation. . . . Do you think I could remember you walking in a furrow behind that Yankee's horse almost barefooted and with your hands blistered—just so the baby and I could have something to eat—and then believe such dreadful things about you? I don't want to hear a word."

Melanie's refusal to believe, or even hear, ill of Scarlett leads Scarlett to passionately desire to keep Melanie's high opinion. It is as Melanie lays dying that Scarlett faces her deep need for Melanie's pure and generous friendship: "Panic clutching at her heart, she knew that Melanie had been her sword and her shield, her comfort and her strength." In two words, Melanie had been her true friend.

A friend loves at all times and always believes the best. Is that the kind of friend you want to have? Is that the kind of friend you aspire to be?

Friendship

Two are better than one; because they have a good reward for their labour. For if they fall, the one will lift up his fellow.

Ecclesiastes 4:9-10 KJV

A friend loves at all times, and a brother is born for adversity.

Proverbs 17:17 NASB

Wounds from a friend are better than many kisses from an enemy.

Proverbs 27:6 NLT

There are friends who pretend to be friends, but there is a friend who sticks closer than a brother.

Proverbs 18:24 RSV

Winning Friends

Dale Carnegie, author of *How To Win Friends and Influence People,* is considered one of the greatest "friend winners" of the century. He taught, "You can make more friends in two months by becoming interested in other people than you can in two years by trying to get other people interested in you."

To illustrate his point, Carnegie would tell how dogs have learned the fine art of making friends better than most people. When you get within ten feet of a friendly dog, he will begin to wag his tail, a visible sign that he welcomes and enjoys your presence. If you take time to pet the dog, he will become excited, lick you, and jump all over you to show how much he appreciates you. The dog became man's best friend by being genuinely interested in people!

One of the foremost ways, of course, in which we show our interest in others is to listen to them—to ask questions, intently listen to their answers, and ask further questions based upon what they say. The person who feels "heard" is likely to seek out his friendly listener again and again, and to count that person as a great friend.

God's Love

And now these three remain: faith, hope and love.
But the greatest of these is love.

1 Corinthians 13:13

Pursue a godly life, along with faith, love,
perseverance, and gentleness.

1 Timothy 6:11 NLT

And above all things have fervent love for one
another, for "love will cover a multitude of sins."

1 Peter 4:8 NKJV

And above all these put on love, which binds
everything together in perfect harmony.

Colossians 3:14 RSV

Jesus Loves Me

A minister received a call from a friend she had not seen in two years. The friend said, "My husband is leaving me for another woman. I need for you to pray with me."

The minister told her friend, "Come quickly."

When her friend arrived, the minister could not help but notice that her friend was carelessly dressed, had gained weight, and had not combed her hair or put on makeup. As they began to converse, the friend admitted to being an uninteresting, nagging wife and a sloppy housekeeper. The minister quickly concluded to herself, *My friend has grown to hate herself!*

When her friend paused to ask for her advice, the minister said only, "Will you join me in a song?" Surprised, her friend agreed. The minister began to sing, "Jesus loves me, this I know." Her friend joined in, tears flooding her eyes. "If Jesus loves me, I must love myself, too," she concluded.

Amazing changes followed. Because she felt loved and lovable, this woman was transformed into the confident woman she once had been. In the process, she recaptured her husband's heart.

We can never accept God's love beyond the degree to which we are willing to love ourselves. Our part is to believe, to receive, and to give.

God's Love

For God so loved the world that he gave his only Son, that whoever believes in him should not perish but have eternal life.

John 3:16 RSV

And he will love thee, and bless thee, and multiply thee.

Deuteronomy 7:13 KJV

The LORD sets prisoners free, the LORD gives sight to the blind, the LORD lifts up those who are bowed down, the LORD loves the righteous.

Psalm 146:7-8

The LORD your God is with you, he is mighty to save. He will take great delight in you, he will quiet you with his love, he will rejoice over you with singing.

Zephaniah 3:17

Adopted to Belong

A Sunday school superintendent was registering two new sisters in Sunday school. She asked their ages and birthdays so she could place them in the appropriate classes. The bolder of the two replied, "We're both seven. My birthday is April 8 and my sister's birthday is April 20." The superintendent replied, "But that's not possible, girls." The quieter sister spoke up. "No, it's true. One of us is adopted."

"Oh?" asked the superintendent. "Which one?" The two sisters looked at each other and smiled. The bolder one said, "We asked Dad that same question awhile ago, but he just looked at us and said he loved us both equally, and he couldn't remember anymore which one of us was adopted."

What a wonderful analogy of God's love! The Apostle Paul wrote to the Romans: "Now if we are [God's] children, then we are heirs—heirs of God and co-heirs with Christ" (Romans 8:17). In essence, as adopted sons and daughters of God, we fully share in the inheritance of His only begotten Son, Jesus. Our Heavenly Father has adopted us and loves us just as much as His beloved Son.

Gossip

Do not spread slanderous gossip among your people.
Leviticus 19:16 NLT

The words of a whisperer are like dainty morsels, and
they go down into the innermost parts of the body.
Proverbs 18:8 NASB

Stay away from gossips—they tell everything.
Proverbs 20:19 CEV

A perverse man stirs up dissension, and a gossip
separates close friends.
Proverbs 16:28

Gossip Golden?

Laura Ingalls Wilder writes in *Little House in the Ozarks:* "I know a little band of friends that calls itself a woman's club. There is no obligation, and there are no promises; but in forming the club and in selecting new members, only those are chosen who are kind-hearted and dependable as well as the possessors of a certain degree of intelligence and a small amount of that genius which is the capacity for careful work. In short, those who are taken into membership are those who will make good friends, and so they are a little band who are each for all and all for each. . . .

"They are getting so in the habit of speaking good words that I expect to see them all develop into Golden Gossips.

"Ever hear of golden gossip? I read of it some years ago. A woman who was always talking about her friends and neighbors made it her business to talk of them, in fact, never said anything but good of them. She was a gossip, but it was 'golden gossip.' This woman's club seems to be working in the same way."

Who wouldn't enjoy belonging to such a club?

Gossip

A gossip betrays a confidence, but a trustworthy man keeps a secret.

Proverbs 11:13

Where there is no wood, the fire goes out; and where there is no talebearer, strife ceases.

Proverbs 26:20 NKJV

Their words are like an open pit, and their tongues are good only for telling lies.

Romans 3:13 CEV

Post a guard at my mouth, GOD, set a watch at the door of my lips.

Psalm 141:3 THE MESSAGE

The Untamed Tongue

Many analogies have been given for the "untamed tongue." Quarles likened it to a drawn sword that takes a person prisoner: "A word unspoken is like the sword in the scabbard, thine; if vented, thy sword is in another's hand."

Others have described evil speaking as:

- A freezing wind—one that seals up the sparkling waters and kills the tender flowers and shoots of growth. In similar fashion, bitter and hate-filled words bind up the hearts of men and cause love to cease to flourish.
- A fox with a firebrand tied to its tail, sent out among the standing corn just as in the days of Samson and the Philistines. So gossip spreads without control or reason.
- A pistol fired in the mountains, the echo of which is intensified until it sounds like thunder.
- A snowball that gathers size as it rolls down a mountain.

Perhaps the greatest analogy, however, is one given by a little child who came running to her mother in tears. "Did your friend hurt you?" the mother asked.

"Yes," said the girl. "Where?" asked her mother.

"Right here," said the child, pointing to her heart.

Ask God to place a watch over your tongue. Your words have the power to hurt and tear down, but they also have the power to heal and build up.

Grief

The LORD therefore said to Moses, "Gather for Me seventy men from the elders of Israel, whom you know to be the elders of the people and their officers and bring them to the tent of meeting, and let them take their stand there with you. Then I will come down and speak with you there, and I will take of the Spirit who is upon you, and will put Him upon them; and they shall bear the burden of the people with you, so that you shall not bear it all alone."

Numbers 11:16-17 NASB

For his anger lasts only a moment, but his favor lasts a lifetime; weeping may remain for a night, but rejoicing comes in the morning.

Psalm 30:5

The LORD has sent me to comfort those who mourn, especially in Jerusalem. He sent me to give them flowers in place of their sorrow, olive oil in place of tears, and joyous praise in place of broken hearts.

Isaiah 61:2-3 CEV

Then Jesus wept.

John 11:35 NLT

A Grief Shared

Some years ago columnist Alexander Woolcott described this scene in a New York hospital:

A mother sat in the hospital lounge in silence, tears streaming down her cheeks. The head nurse comforted her about the death, just moments before, of her only child.

The nurse asked her, "Did you see the little boy sitting in the hall as you left your daughter's room?" No, the mother said, she had not noticed him.

His mother had been brought to the hospital by ambulance a few days earlier. Recent immigrants, they knew no one in the city. Every day and night the little boy sat outside his mother's room.

"Fifteen minutes ago that little boy's mother died," the nurse continued, "and now I must go tell this child that he is all alone in the world."

Then the nurse added, "I don't suppose you would go with me?"

The grieving mother looked up in shock, but dried her tears, straightened her hair, and went with the nurse. Not only that, she put her arms around the boy and invited him to come home with her.

They soon came to know the meaning of the promise: A grief shared is a burden lightened.

Grief

And God will wipe away every tear from their eyes; there shall be no more death, nor sorrow, nor crying. There shall be no more pain.

Revelation 21:4 NKJV

Weeping may remain for a night, but rejoicing comes in the morning.

Psalm 30:5

He heals the heartbroken and bandages their wounds.

Psalm 147:3 THE MESSAGE

Everything on earth has its own time and its own season. . . . for crying and laughing, weeping and dancing.

Ecclesiastes 3:1,4 CEV

God Grieves with You

In *Women Who Do Too Much,* Patricia Sprinkle writes: "Three months before I spoke with Nancy, her husband lost a four-year battle to a degenerative brain disease. She said, 'This was a brilliant man, a gentle man, a man with a terrific sense of humor. I grieved as he lost his ability to walk, pick up things from the floor, write, speak clearly. We had been married for thirty years and expected to grow old together. Suddenly, in one day, our life changed. He flew to Mayo Clinic one morning and called me that night with the doctor's diagnosis. They could do nothing for him.

"'I remember thinking after I hung up the phone, life is never going to be the same again. Nobody gets a rehearsal for this. You don't get to practice.

"'I was furious with God—banged my fist on many tables. But I learned to thank God that God is God. God didn't get bowled over by my fury. Instead, He told me, "I won't leave you. I'm as sad about this as you are. I grieve with you." The shared grief of God gets me through my own.'"

Jesus called the Holy Spirit the "Comforter." He is with us every moment of our lives.

Guidance

For this God is our God for ever and ever; he will be our guide even to the end.

Psalm 48:14

A man's heart deviseth his way: but the LORD directeth his steps.

Proverbs 16:9 KJV

Stalwart walks in step with GOD; his path blazed by GOD, he's happy.

Psalm 37:23 THE MESSAGE

The LORD says, "I will guide you along the best pathway for your life. I will advise you and watch over you."

Psalm 32:8 NLT

The Guide

In *A Slow and Certain Light,* Elisabeth Elliot
writes: "When I lived in the forest of Ecuador I
usually traveled on foot. . . . Trails often led
through streams and rivers, but sometimes there was
a log high above the water which we had to cross.

"I dreaded those logs and was always
tempted to take the steep, hard way down into the
ravine and up the other side. But the Indians
would say, 'Just walk across, señorita,' and over
they would go, light-footed and confident. I was
barefoot as they were, but it was not enough. On
the log, I couldn't keep from looking down at the
river below. I knew I would slip. I had never been
any good at balancing myself . . . so my guide
would stretch out a hand, and the touch of it was
all I needed. I stopped worrying about slipping. I
stopped looking down at the river or even at the
log and looked at the guide, who held my hand
with only the lightest touch. When I reached the
other side, I realized that if I had slipped he could
not have held me. But his being there and his
touch were all I needed."

God is your guide, go on with peace and
confidence that He will hold you up.

Guidance

And the Lord will guide you continually and satisfy your desire with good things, and make your bones strong; and you shall be like a watered garden, like a spring of water, whose waters fail not.

Isaiah 58:11 RSV

When the Holy Spirit, who is truth, comes, he shall guide you into all truth, for he will not be presenting his own ideas, but will be passing on to you what he has heard. He will tell you about the future.

John 16:13 TLB

But he led his own people like a flock of sheep, guiding them safely through the wilderness.

Psalm 78:52 NLT

For all who are led by the Spirit of God are sons of God.

Romans 8:14 RSV

Reference Point

In his book, *The Final Week of Jesus,* Max Lucado tells this story of where to look when you feel lost:

"One of the reference points of London is the Charing Cross. It is near the geographical center of the city and serves as a navigational tool for those confused by the streets.

"A little girl was lost in the great city. A policeman found her. Between sobs and tears, she explained she didn't know her way home. He asked her if she knew her address. She didn't. He asked her phone number; she didn't know that either. But when he asked her what she knew, suddenly her face lit up.

"'I know the Cross,' she said. 'Show me the Cross and I can find my way home from there.'"

When you need guidance and direction, look to the Cross. Jesus Christ provided everything we need there. And when He arose and ascended into heaven, He sent us the Holy Spirit to walk beside us and show us the way.

Throughout the Bible, God promises us that our steps are directed by Him. When we put our trust in Him and rely on the Holy Spirit, we will never fail to find our way.

Happiness

How blessed is the one whom You choose, and bring near to You, to dwell in Your courts.

Psalm 65:4 NASB

It is possible to give freely and become more wealthy, but those who are stingy will lose everything.

Proverbs 11:24 NLT

A generous man will himself be blessed, for he shares his food with the poor.

Proverbs 22:9

Warn the rich people of this world not to be proud or to trust in wealth that is easily lost. Tell them to have faith in God, who is rich and blesses us with everything we need to enjoy life. Instruct them to do as many good deeds as they can and to help everyone. Remind the rich to be generous and share what they have. This will lay a solid foundation for the future, so that they will know what true life is like.

1 Timothy 6:17-19 CEV

The Secret of Happiness

One day, feeling especially sad and lonely, a little girl named Sabrina took a walk through a meadow, where she noticed a small butterfly caught by its wings on a sharp thorn bush. Carefully, Sabrina released it. Suddenly, the butterfly changed into a lovely good fairy.

"For your wonderful kindness," the good fairy said to Sabrina, "I will tell you the secret of happiness." The fairy whispered something in her ear, and then vanished.

As Sabrina grew up, everyone loved to be around her, and often coaxed her to tell them the secret of her happiness. She would tell about the fairy, but never about the secret.

Finally, when she was very old and on her deathbed, Sabrina gathered the neighbors around her and told them, "I do not want the secret of happiness to die with me, and so I will tell it to you. "Tell us, tell us," they pleaded.

"She told me that everyone, no matter how old or young, rich or poor, no matter how secure they seemed, would have need of me."

The desire to be needed is one of humanity's greatest needs. If you can find ways for people to be needed by others, you will find lasting happiness for yourself.

Happiness

Is any one among you suffering? Let him pray. Is any cheerful? Let him sing praise.

James 5:13 RSV

I will bless the LORD at all times; His praise shall continually be in my mouth.

Psalm 34:1 NKJV

Rejoice in the Lord always. I will say it again: Rejoice!

Philippians 4:4

Behold, we call those happy who were steadfast. You have heard of the steadfastness of Job, and you have seen the purpose of the Lord, how the Lord is compassionate and merciful.

James 5:11 RSV

The World Won't Make You Happy

When the great golfer Babe Didrikson Zaharias was dying of cancer, her husband, George Zaharias, came to her bedside. Although he desired to be strong for her sake, he found he was unable to control his emotions and began to cry. Babe said to him gently, "Now honey, don't take on so. While I've been in the hospital, I have learned one thing. A moment of happiness is a lifetime, and I have had a lot of happiness."

Happiness does not come wrapped in brightly colored packages as a "gift" given to us by others. Happiness comes when we uncover the gifts that lie within us and begin to use them to please God and bless others.

Happiness flows from within. It is found in the moments of life we label as "quality" rather than quantity. George Bernard Shaw once said, "This is the true joy in life: Being used for a purpose recognized by yourself as a mighty one. . . . Being a force of nature instead of a feverish, selfish, little clod of ailments and grievances, complaining that the world will not devote itself to making you happy."

The only person who can truly make you happy is yourself. You simply have to decide to be.

Health

Yes, I will bless the Lord and not forget the glorious things he does for me. He forgives all my sins. He heals me.

Psalm 103:2-3 TLB

Surely he took up our infirmities and carried our sorrows, yet we considered him stricken by God, smitten by him, and afflicted. But he was pierced for our transgressions, he was crushed for our iniquities; the punishment that brought us peace was upon him, and by his wounds we are healed.

Isaiah 53:4-5

And ye shall serve the LORD your God, and he shall bless thy bread, and thy water; and I will take sickness away from the midst of thee. There shall nothing cast their young, nor be barren, in thy land: the number of thy days I will fulfil.

Exodus 23:25-26 KJV

Heal me, O LORD, and I shall be healed; save me, and I shall be saved: for thou art my praise.

Jeremiah 17:14 KJV

Standing in the Gap

A young woman lay in a hospital, far from home and family, drifting in and out of consciousness. Several times she became aware of a woman's voice praying for her salvation, as well as for her physical healing. At one point, a physician described her condition as critical, warning those present in the room that she might not survive. Then she heard a second voice, one that spoke in faith: "Doctor, I respect what you say, but I cannot accept it. I've been praying and I believe she will not only recover, but she will walk out of here and live for God."

Before long, the young woman did walk out of that hospital and return to work. It was then she learned that it had been her boss's wife (whom she had met only twice) who had stood in the gap, interceding for her at her hospital bed. When she attempted to thank this woman for her prayers, she replied, "Don't thank me, thank God. Others have prayed for me. Their prayers changed my life."

It was five more years before the young woman gave her life to Christ, but all the while, she never forgot how a faithful woman of God had believed He was faithful to heal.

Health

I am the LORD who heals you.
Exodus 15:26 NLT

He spoke the word that healed you, that pulled you back from the brink of death.
Psalm 107:20 THE MESSAGE

My son, give attention to my words; incline your ear to my sayings. For they are life to those who find them, and health to all their body.
Proverbs 4:20,22 NASB

And all the crowd sought to touch him, for power came forth from him and healed them all.
Luke 6:19 RSV

A Healthy Dose of Words

It takes just as much energy to say a positive word as it does a negative one. In fact, it may actually take less. Research has shown that when we speak positive words—even in difficult circumstances or troubling situations—we become relaxed. As we relax, the flow of blood to the brain increases. A well-oxygenated brain can think more creatively, make wise decisions, find reasonable solutions, and generate pertinent answers.

Positive words ease relationships and create an atmosphere of peace that is conducive to rest, relaxation, and rejuvenation—all of which are necessary for good health.

A continual flow of negative words causes relationships to suffer, which creates an atmosphere of disharmony and makes for fitful sleep and frayed nerves—none of which are healthy!

Negative thoughts and words keep the body in a state of tension, constricting muscles and blood vessels, which often causes irrational and uncharacteristic behavior.

God desires for us to walk in the health He has provided for us in the death, burial, and resurrection of Jesus. One of the ways we can do that is to watch what we say. And in order to watch what we say, we must watch what we think. Push away negative thoughts and think positively!

Hope

Praise be to the God and Father of our Lord Jesus Christ! In his great mercy he has given us new birth into a living hope through the resurrection of Jesus Christ from the dead, and into an inheritance that can never perish, spoil or fade— kept in heaven for you.

1 Peter 1:3

O Lord, you alone are my hope. I've trusted you, O LORD, from childhood.

Psalm 71:5 NLT

When they see me waiting, expecting your Word, those who fear you will take heart and be glad.

Psalm 119:74 THE MESSAGE

Hope in God and wait expectantly for Him, for I shall yet praise Him, my Help and my God.

Psalm 42:5 AMP

God is Real

Dr. Walter Eerdman wrote a best-seller some years ago entitled *Source of Power in Famous Lives*. In it, he gave biographical sketches of fifty great men and women of history—among them David Livingstone, Jenny Lind, Clara Barton, Frances Willard, Christopher Columbus, and Oliver Cromwell.

Eerdman drew this conclusion about the people he had profiled: "In their lives, God was a reality."

Truly great people share a common source of power—they simply apply that power in different ways. Some have greater public success and thus attain to a greater degree of fame and prominence than others. Many less famous people, however, have also encouraged others with their stories of personal triumphs and victories. This shows that the power that comes from having a real relationship with God isn't limited to the rich and famous. It can be attained by anyone, regardless of his or her wealth or position in society.

Genuine power from God is manifest as hope in times of disaster, calm in times of crises, direction in times of confusion, and an enduring faith in times of fear. Anyone can know this power if they will put their hope in God and allow Him to become a reality in their lives.

Hope

I wipe away your sins because of who I am. And so, I will forget the wrongs you have done.

Isaiah 43:25 CEV

As far as sunrise is from sunset, he has separated us from our sins.

Psalm 103:12 THE MESSAGE

All that the Father gives me will come to me, and whoever comes to me I will never drive away.

John 6:37

Most assuredly, I say to you, he who hears My word and believes in Him who sent Me has everlasting life, and shall not come into judgment, but has passed from death into life.

John 5:24 NKJV

Hope from the Flowers

The fictional character Sherlock Holmes is known for his keen powers of observation in solving crimes. But Holmes also used his skills for renewing his faith. In *The Adventure of the Naval Treaty*, Dr. Watson says of Holmes: "He walked past the couch to an open window and held up the drooping stalk of a moss rose, looking down at the dainty blend of crimson and green. It was a new phase of his character to me, for I had never before seen him show an interest in natural objects.

"'There is nothing in which deduction is so necessary as in religion,' said he, leaning with his back against the shutters. . . . 'Our highest assurance of the goodness of Providence seems to me to rest in the flowers. All other things, our powers, our desires, our food, are really necessary for our existence in the first instance. But this rose is an extra. Its smell and its color are an embellishment of life, not a condition of it. It is only goodness which gives extras, and so I say again that we have much to hope from the flowers.'"

Life is filled with these "extras"—gifts from a loving God that enrich our lives and assure us of His great love.

Hospitality

In all things I have shown you that by so toiling one must help the weak, remembering the words of the Lord Jesus, how he said, "It is more blessed to give than to receive."

Acts 20:35 RSV

When God's children are in need, be the one to help them out. And get into the habit of inviting guests home for dinner or, if they need lodging, for the night.

Romans 12:13 NLT

Be hospitable to one another without grumbling.

1 Peter 4:9 NKJV

Dear children, let us not love with words or tongue but with actions and in truth.

1 John 3:18

Home Sweet Home

In *Secret Strength,* Joni Eareckson Tada writes a wonderful tribute to a genuine "home sweet home":

"Not long ago I entered a friend's home and immediately sensed the glory of God. No, that impression was not based on some heebie-jeebie feeling or super-spiritual instinct. And it had nothing to do with several Christian plaques I spotted hanging in the hallway. Yet there was a peace and orderliness that pervaded that home. Joy and music hung in the air. Although the kids were normal, active youngsters, everyone's activity seemed to dovetail together, creating the impression that the home had direction, that the kids really cared about each other, that the parents put love into action.

"We didn't even spend that much time 'fellowshipping' in the usual sense of the word— talking about the Bible or praying together. Yet we laughed. And really heard each other. And opened our hearts like family members. After dinner I left that home refreshed. It was a place where God's essential being was on display. His kindness, His love, His justice. It was filled with God's glory."

Real hospitality is more than pretty dishes and fancy centerpieces. It is inviting God's presence into our home and then sharing His peace and love with others.

Hospitality

Cheerfully share your home with those who need a meal or a place to stay for the night. God has given each of you some special abilities; be sure to use them to help each other.

1 Peter 4:9-10 TLB

Be not forgetful to entertain strangers: for thereby some have entertained angels unawares.

Hebrews 13:2 KJV

We ought therefore to show hospitality to such men so that we may work together for the truth.

3 John 8

Behold, I stand at the door and knock; if anyone hears My voice and opens the door, I will come in to him and will dine with him, and he with Me.

Revelation 3:20 NASB

Friends Don't Let Friends Eat Alone

Here's a great place to find an example of friendly, warm hospitality—the story of Winnie the Pooh.

One day Winnie the Pooh decided to go for a walk in the Hundred-Acre Wood. It's about 11:30 in the morning, just before lunch—a fine time to go walking.

Pooh sets off across the stream, stepping on the stones, and when he gets right in the middle of the stream, he sits down on a warm rock and thinks about which of his friends would be the best one to visit.

"I think I'll go see Tigger," he says to himself. Then he remembers that Tigger is in a bad mood.

"Owl," he thinks. Then, "No, Owl uses big words, hard-to-understand words."

At last, he brightens up.

"I know! I think I'll go see Rabbit. I like Rabbit. Rabbit uses encouraging words like, 'How's about lunch?' and 'Help yourself to some more, Pooh!' Yes, I think I'll go see Rabbit."

Which kind of host are you? Are you moody like Tigger? Are you condescending like Owl? Or, do you use encouraging, hospitable words like Rabbit?

Integrity

Till I die, I will not deny my integrity.
Job 27:5

And as for you, if you will walk before me, as David your father walked, with integrity of heart and uprightness, doing according to all that I have commanded you, and keeping my statutes and my ordinances, then I will establish your royal throne over Israel for ever, as I promised.
1 Kings 9:4-5 RSV

When the storm has swept by, the wicked are gone, but the righteous stand firm forever.
Proverbs 10:25

By standing firm you will gain life.
Luke 21:19

The Hallmark of Integrity

Dwight L. Moody's father died when Dwight was only four. With nine mouths to feed and no income, the widow Moody was dogged by creditors. In response to the situation, the eldest son ran away from home. Few would have criticized Mrs. Moody for seeking assistance or letting others help raise her children. However, she was determined to keep her family together.

On a nightly basis, Mrs. Moody placed a light in the window, certain her son would return home. Dwight wrote of those days, "When the wind was very high and the house would tremble at every gust, the voice of my mother was raised in prayer." In time, her prayers were answered. Moody recalls that no one recognized his older brother when he came to the door, a great beard flowed down his chest. It was only as the tears began to soak his beard that Mrs. Moody recognized her son and invited him in. He said, "No, Mother, I will not come in until I hear first that you have forgiven me." She was only too willing to forgive, of course, and threw her arms around her son in a warm embrace.

Mrs. Moody didn't change just because her circumstances did. That is the hallmark of integrity.

Integrity

Who may stay in God's temple or live on the holy mountain of the LORD? Only those who obey God and do as they should. They speak the truth and don't spread gossip; they treat others fairly and don't say cruel things.

Psalm 15:1-2 CEV

He is the Rock, His work is perfect; for all His ways are justice, a God of truth and without injustice; righteous and upright is He.

Deuteronomy 32:4 NKJV

Buy truth, and do not sell it, get wisdom and instruction and understanding.

Proverbs 23:23 NASB

Therefore each of you must put off falsehood and speak truthfully to his neighbor, for we are all members of one body.

Ephesians 4:25

A National Champion
in the Honesty Bee

Rosalie Elliott had made it to the fourth round of a national spelling contest in Washington. The eleven-year-old from South Carolina had been asked to spell the word *avowal*. In her soft southern accent she spelled the word, but the judges were not able to determine if she had used an *a* or an *e* as the next to last letter. They debated among themselves for several minutes as they listened to tape recording playbacks. The crucial letter, however, was too accent-blurred to decipher.

Finally the chief judge put the question to the only person who knew the answer. "Was the letter an *a* or was it an *e?*" he asked Rosalie.

By this time Rosalie had heard the correct spelling. Still, without hesitation, she replied that she had misspelled the word.

The entire audience stood and applauded, including some fifty news reporters. Even in defeat, she was a victor. Few remember the name of the first-place winner that year, but the name of Rosalie Elliott is passed down wherever stories about truthfulness are told.

Imagine the heartwarming and proud moment for Rosalie's parents! Our tests of truthfulness may not be quite so public, but we should practice it in our ordinary family conversations.

Jealousy

For where you have envy and selfish ambition,
there you find disorder and every evil practice.
James 3:16

Be still before the LORD and wait patiently for
him; do not fret when men succeed in their ways,
when they carry out their wicked schemes.
Psalm 37:7

If we live by the Spirit, let us also walk by the Spirit.
Let us have no self-conceit, no provoking of one
another, no envy of one another.
Galatians 5:25-26 RSV

You shall not covet your neighbor's house. You
shall not covet your neighbor's wife, or his
manservant or maidservant, his ox or donkey, or
anything that belongs to your neighbor.
Exodus 20:17

Different, but the Same

At the height of the segregation storm in the United States, a six-year-old girl headed out for her first day of school. Her elementary school was one that had been integrated recently, and the community was still full of tension. After school her mother met her anxiously at the door, eager to hear how the day had gone. "Did everything go all right, honey?" she asked.

"Oh, Mother! You know what?" the little girl said eagerly, "A little black girl sat next to me."

With growing apprehension the mother asked, "And what happened?"

The little girl replied, "We were both so scared about our first day at school that we held hands all day."

Often, jealousy and hate are born out of a lack of information—we simply don't know a person or an individual member of a group. Once we discover the many things that we share in common with another person—including our fears, our hopes, our concerns, our desires—our differences simply enhance our relationships.

When we allow one another our unique differences, jealousy fades and love grows.

Jealousy

Do not fret because of evil men or be envious of those who do wrong.

Psalm 37:1

Love is patient, love is kind. It does not envy, it does not boast, it is not proud.

1 Corinthians 13:4

You shall not covet.

Exodus 20:17 NKJV

Wrath is fierce and anger is a flood, but who can stand before jealousy?

Proverbs 27:4 NASB

Focus on What You Have

Good Morning America former co-host Joan Lunden recalls, "When I first came on [the] program in 1978, hosting with David Hartman, he got to interview all the celebrities and politicians and kings. I got the information spots. . . . I received piles of letters from women who were unhappy that I was allowing myself to be used in this way. Well, the fact was I enjoyed those spots and I was good at them. I had to accept that it was either that way or no way at all.

"I can't see any reason to spend your time frustrated, angry, or upset about things you don't have or you can't have or you can't yet do. I drill this into my children when I hear them say, 'I don't have this.' I'll say, 'Don't focus on what you don't have. Focus on what you do have and be grateful for it. Be proud of what you can do. Those things you can't do yet, maybe you will do.'"

When we are jealous of others who have gifts and talents that we don't, we get nowhere. God never asks us to become something that we aren't, all He asks is that we use the gifts He's given us to the best of our ability.

Joy

May those who sow in tears reap with shouts of joy! He that goes forth weeping, bearing the seed for sowing, shall come home with shouts of joy, bringing his sheaves with him.

Psalm 126:5-6 RSV

So you have sorrow now, but I will see you again and your hearts will rejoice, and no one will take your joy from you.

John 16:22 RSV

Yes, the gladness you have given me is far greater than their joys at harvest time as they gaze at their bountiful crops.

Psalm 4:7 TLB

Then he said to them, "Go your way, eat the fat and drink sweet wine and send portions to him for whom nothing is prepared; for this day is holy to our LORD; and do not be grieved, for the joy of the LORD is your strength."

Nehemiah 8:10 RSV

The Joy of Little Cranberry Island

Joy Sprague knows how to brighten the days of her customers. As the postmaster for Little Cranberry Island, Maine, she actually has customers competing to get their pictures on her post office wall. Every twenty-fifth customer to use the U.S. Postal Service's Express Mail has a "mug shot" taken which is hung on the wall. They also receive a plate of Joy's home-baked cream puffs!

That's not all Joy does to make Little Cranberry, population 90, a friendlier place. She operates a mail-order stamp business that is so popular her tiny post office ranks fourth in sales out of 450 outlets in Maine. Why? Most of Joy's customers are summer visitors who want to stay up to date with the news of the island. Along with each order, Joy sends a snapshot of an island scene and a handwritten note about island events.

One of the residents has remarked, "She invents ways to bring pleasure to others." Joy has received praise from the U.S. Postmaster General and has the warm affection not only of the local residents, but friends across America who delight in corresponding with her.

Why not ask the Lord to give you creative ideas which will bring joy to someone's life today?

Joy

My soul is feasted as with marrow and fat, and my mouth praises thee with joyful lips, when I think of thee upon my bed, and meditate on thee in the watches of the night.

Psalm 63:5-6 RSV

You have given me greater joy than those who have abundant harvests of grain and wine.

Psalm 4:7 NLT

We cried as we went out to plant our seeds. Now let us celebrate as we bring in the crops. We cried on the way to plant our seeds, but we will celebrate and shout as we bring in the crops.

Psalm 126:5-6 CEV

Now is your time of grief, but I will see you again and you will rejoice, and no one will take away your joy.

John 16:22

Overflowing Joy

One day during her morning devotions, Jeannie found herself weeping as she read Psalm 139:23, "Search me, O God, and know my heart." She cried out to the Lord to cleanse her of several bad attitudes she had been harboring. Later that morning as she boarded an airplane, she had a strong feeling that God was confirming to her that He had forgiven her and could now use her for a special assignment. She whispered a prayer, "Lord, help me to stay awake."

Jeannie usually took motion-sickness medication before flying, and therefore, often slept from takeoff to landing. On this flight, however, she forced herself to stay awake. A woman took the seat next to her on the flight and as they began to talk, the woman asked, "Why do you have so much joy?" Jeannie replied, "Because of Jesus." And for the next three hours, she had a wonderful opportunity to witness to the woman. Later, she sent her a Bible and they exchanged letters. Then late one evening, the woman called and Jeannie led her to the Lord over the phone.

The Lord will not only hear your heart's cry today, but His answer will fill you with overflowing joy that you will be able to share with others.

Justice

God presented him as a sacrifice of atonement, through faith in his blood. He did this to demonstrate his justice, because in his forbearance he had left the sins committed beforehand unpunished.

Romans 3:25

The Lord has made himself known, he has executed judgment; the wicked are snared in the work of their own hands.

Psalm 9:16 RSV

Let true justice prevail, so you may live and occupy the land that the LORD your God is giving you.

Deuteronomy 16:20 NLT

The king's strength also loveth judgment; thou dost establish equity, thou executest judgment and righteousness in Jacob.

Psalm 99:4 KJV

Justice and Mercy

One of New York City's most popular mayors was Fiorello LaGuardia. Nearly every older New Yorker has a favorite memory of him. Some recall the day he read the funny papers over the radio, with all the appropriate inflections, because a strike had kept the Sunday newspapers off the stands.

One time, the mayor chose to preside in a night court. An old woman was brought before him on that bitterly cold night. The charge was stealing a loaf of bread. She explained that her family was starving. LaGuardia replied, "I've got to punish you. The law makes no exception. I must fine you ten dollars." At that, he reached into his own pocket and pulled out a ten-dollar bill. "Well," he said, "here's the ten dollars to pay your fine, which I now remit." He then tossed the ten-dollar bill into his own hat and declared, "I'm going to fine everybody in this courtroom fifty cents for living in a town where a person has to steal bread in order to eat. Mr. Bailiff, collect the fines and give them to this defendant."

After the hat was passed, the incredulous old woman left the courtroom with a new light in her eyes and $47.50 in her pocket to buy groceries! That's God's kind of justice!

Justice

But let him who glories glory in this, that he understands and knows me, that I am the Lord who practices steadfast love, justice, and right-eousness in the earth; for in these things I delight.

Jeremiah 9:24 RSV

He does not crush the weak, or quench the smallest hope; he will end all conflict with his final victory, and his name shall be the hope of all the world.

Matthew 12:20-21 TLB

Instead, I want to see a mighty flood of justice, a river of righteous living that will never run dry.

Amos 5:24 NLT

He has shown you, O man, what is good; and what does the LORD require of you but to do justly, to love mercy, and to walk humbly with your God?

Micah 6:8 NKJV

Eternal Harmony

Centuries ago, a certain tribal leader was known for his great wisdom. In order to help his people live safely and peacefully, he carefully put laws into place guiding every aspect of tribal life.

In spite of those laws, there were problems. One day it came to the leader's attention that someone in the tribe was stealing.

"You know that the laws are for your protection, to help you live safely and in peace," he reminded them. "This stealing must stop.

"The penalty has been increased from ten to twenty lashes from the whip for the person caught stealing."

But the thief continued to steal. The leader increased the penalty until finally, it was forty lashes. Then a man came to say that the thief had been caught.

When the thief was bought to him the leader's face fell in shock and grief. It was his very own mother, old and frail.

The leader spoke, "It is for our safety and peace. There must be forty lashes." The guards led his mother forward and one began to unwind his whip.

At the same moment, the leader stepped forward and wrapped his arms around his mother, shielding her with his own body.

A single moment, yet in it love and justice found an eternal harmony.

Loneliness

Height nor depth, nor any other created thing,
shall be able to separate us from the love of God
which is in Christ Jesus our Lord.

Romans 8:39 NKJV

The eternal God is thy refuge, and underneath are
the everlasting arms.

Deuteronomy 33:27 KJV

Be still, and know that I am God; I will be exalted
among the nations, I will be exalted in the earth.

Psalm 46:10

For you are my hiding place; you protect me from
trouble. You surround me with songs of victory.

Psalm 32:7 NLT

Don't Go It Alone

A woman was in a serious automobile accident in a city far from home. She felt so enclosed in a cocoon of pain, she didn't realize how lonely she was until a "forgotten" friend in the city came to visit her. Her friend firmly, but gently said to her, "You should not be alone."

In the weeks that followed, this friend's advice rang in the injured woman's ears and helped her to overcome her otherwise reserved nature. When another friend called from a city several hundred miles away to say she wanted to come stay with her, the injured woman didn't say, "Don't bother"—as would have been her normal response. Instead, she said, "Please come." The friend was a wonderful encouragement to her. Then, yet another friend offered to come and help in her recovery. Again she swallowed her pride and said, "Please do." This friend stayed for several months until the injured woman was able to care for herself.

Even Jesus did not carry His own cross all the way to Calvary. He allowed another to help shoulder His burden. It's all right to ask for help and to receive help. You don't have to "go it alone." Let a friend help you!

Loneliness

Behold, I am with you and will keep you wherever
you go, and will bring you back to this land; for I
will not leave you until I have done that of which
I have spoken to you.

Genesis 28:15 RSV

All those who know your mercy, Lord, will count
on you for help. For you have never yet forsaken
those who trust in you.

Psalm 9:10 TLB

I will never fail you. I will never forsake you.

Hebrews 13:5 NLT

God sets the lonely in families, he leads forth the
prisoners with singing.

Psalm 68:6

Get Going!

In her book *Lifelines,* Lynn Caine, a widow who struggles with loneliness and isolation, seeks to offer solutions to others in similar situations. She identifies with those who are wallowing in self-pity, and with those who are trying too hard to find someone to fill the vacuum in their lives.

She offers a simple prescription to loneliness that helped alleviate her own depression. "The only solution is to strengthen oneself. And here is where those courses and committees, sports and crafts can play an important role. They can help a woman grow. If you join a tennis club or study accounting or go on early-morning bird walks because you think you will meet a man or make a friend, the chances are you won't.

But if you have always wanted to understand the stock market, have dreamed of being a real estate agent, then go to it. Enroll in a class; join a club; follow your interests. If you are passionate about saving the whales, building dollhouses, running for political office . . . get going. Get involved. You may meet like-minded souls and make lifetime friends, or you may not. But you will be less lonely because you will be more interesting—and stronger."

Love

Though I speak with the tongues of men and of angels, and have not charity, I am become as sounding brass, or a tinkling cymbal.

1 Corinthians 13:1 KJV

If I had the gift of prophecy, and if I knew all the mysteries of the future and knew everything about everything, but didn't love others, what good would I be? And if I had the gift of faith so that I could speak to a mountain and make it move, without love I would be no good to anybody.

1 Corinthians 13:2 NLT

What if I gave away all that I owned and let myself be burned alive? I would gain nothing, unless I loved others.

1 Corinthians 13:3 CEV

Love is patient, love is kind. It does not envy, it does not boast, it is not proud. It is not rude, it is not self-seeking, it is not easily angered, it keeps no record of wrongs. Love does not delight in evil but rejoices with the truth. It always protects, always trusts, always hopes, always perseveres.

1 Corinthians 13:4-7

Life-Transforming Love

The poet Robert Browning met the love of his life, Elizabeth Barrett, when both were over forty years old. During her early years, Elizabeth had endured hell on earth. One of eleven children, she grew up under the siege of an oppressive, abusive father. His angry rages frequently confined her to bed with an accumulation of ills.

Then Elizabeth met Robert. He did not see her as a sickly, middle-aged invalid, but as a beautiful, talented spirit waiting to bloom. After some brutal confrontations with her father, they were married and traveled the European continent, drinking in the wonders of centuries-old beauty.

Their union transformed them both. At forty-three, Elizabeth gave birth to her first child. This loving wife and mother at last began to explore her gift for poetry. The collections she wrote, such as *Sonnets from the Portuguese,* celebrate in word portraits the transformation of her life. One of the poems included was the incomparable "How Do I Love Thee?"

The Elizabeth Barrett Browning who became one of our greatest romantic poets was there all the time, just waiting for her lover to discover her. Is someone in your life waiting for your love to bring out the best in them?

Love

Your cheeks are beautiful with earrings, your neck with strings of jewels. We will make you earrings of gold, studded with silver.

Song of Songs 1:10-11

You have ravished my heart, my treasure, my bride. I am overcome by one glance of your eyes, by a single bead of your necklace. How sweet is your love, my treasure, my bride! How much better it is than wine! Your perfume is more fragrant than the richest of spices.

Song of Songs 4:9-10 NLT

I went down to see if blossoms were on the walnut trees, grapevines, and fruit trees. But in my imagination I was suddenly riding on a glorious chariot.

Song of Songs 6:11-12 CEV

Put me like a seal over your heart, like a seal on your arm. For love is as strong as death, jealousy is as severe as Sheol; its flashes are flashes of fire, the very flame of the LORD.

Song of Songs 8:6 NASB

How Do I Love Thee?

How do I love thee? Let me count the ways.
I love thee to the depth and breadth and height
My soul can reach, when feeling out of sight
For the ends of Being and ideal Grace.
I love thee to the level of everyday's
Most quiet need, by sun and candlelight.
I love thee freely, as men strive for Right;
I love thee purely, as they turn from Praise.
I love thee with the passion put to use
In my old griefs, and with my childhood's faith.
I love thee with a love I seemed to lose
With my lost saints!—I love thee with the breath,
Smiles, tears, all of my life!—and if God choose,
I shall but love thee better after death.

Elizabeth Barrett Browning

As you read the words of this immortal love poem, consider how you would "count the ways" you might describe the love of your life. In silence, picture images of your beloved—at work, at play, alone, with you, with your children, in laughter, at prayer. Sometimes words will be given to you, just when you think words cannot express your feelings. Feel free to write them and show them to him.

Marriage

And the LORD God said, It is not good that the man should be alone; I will make him an help meet for him.

Genesis 2:18 KJV

Therefore what God has joined together, let man not separate.

Matthew 19:6

He who finds a wife finds what is good and receives favor from the LORD.

Proverbs 18:22

But I want you to understand that the head of every man is Christ, the head of a woman is her husband, and the head of Christ is God.

1 Corinthians 11:3 RSV

Promises

In Thornton Wilder's play *The Skin of Our Teeth,* the character Mrs. Antrobus says to her husband, "I didn't marry you because you were perfect. . . . I married you because you gave me a promise."

She then takes off her ring and looks at it, saying, "That promise made up for your faults and the promise I gave you made up for mine. Two imperfect people got married, and it was the promise that made the marriage."

In every marriage, no matter how well the two people know one another, great mysteries remain! Very often, each person comes to the marriage

- not fully knowing himself or herself,
- not fully knowing about life, and
- not fully knowing about his or her spouse.

What is unknown is far greater than what is known!

Becoming a faithful, loving spouse not only takes courage and faith, but patience and a desire to keep learning and growing. Better than asking, "What kind of spouse do I desire to have?" is the question, "What kind of spouse do I aspire to be?"

Marriage

Be subject to one another out of reverence for Christ.
Ephesians 5:21 RSV

Wives, submit to your husbands as to the Lord.
Ephesians 5:22

And you husbands must love your wives with the same love Christ showed the church. He gave up his life for her.
Ephesians 5:25 NLT

As the Scriptures say, "A man leaves his father and mother to get married, and he becomes like one person with his wife."
Ephesians 5:31 CEV

Age Before Beauty

From German pastor and theologian Helmut Thielicke comes this beautiful picture of a marriage where love has continued to grow through the years:

"I once knew a very old married couple who radiated a profound happiness. The wife, especially, who was almost unable to move because of her age and illness, possessed a kind face, etched with a hundred lines by the joys and sufferings of many years. She exhibited such a gratitude for life that I was touched to the quick.

"I asked myself what could possibly be the source of this kindly person's radiance. In so many respects they were quite ordinary people, and their home indicated only the most modest comforts.

"Suddenly I saw where it all came from. I saw these two speaking to each other, and their eyes hanging upon each other. It became clear to me that this woman was dearly loved.

"It was not that she was loved all those years by her husband because she was a cheerful and pleasant person. It was the other way around. Because she was so loved, she became the person I saw before me."

In your marriage, you can enjoy a lifelong relationship with your beloved. "Because he is so loved" by you.

Obedience

If you listen to these regulations and obey them faithfully, the LORD your God will keep his covenant of unfailing love with you, as he solemnly promised your ancestors.

Deuteronomy 7:12 NLT

If you keep my commands, you'll remain intimately at home in my love. That's what I've done—kept my Father's commands and made myself at home in his love.

John 15:10 THE MESSAGE

When we obey God, we are sure that we know him. We truly love God only when we obey him as we should, and then we know that we belong to him.

1 John 2:3,5 CEV

Dear friends, if our hearts do not condemn us, we have confidence before God and receive from him anything we ask, because we obey his commands and do what pleases him.

1 John 3:21-22

Obeying God's Call

In *Dakota*, Kathleen Norris writes: "A Benedictine sister from the Philippines once told me what her community did when some sisters took to the streets in the popular revolt against the Marcos regime. Some did not think it proper for nuns to demonstrate in public, let alone risk arrest. In a group meeting that began and ended with prayer, the sisters who wished to continue demonstrating explained that this was for them a religious obligation; those who disapproved also had their say. Everyone spoke; everyone heard and gave counsel.

"It was eventually decided that the nuns who were demonstrating should continue to do so; those who wished to express solidarity but were unable to march would prepare food and provide medical assistance to the demonstrators, and those who disapproved would pray for everyone. The sisters laughed and said, 'If one of the conservative sisters was praying that we young, crazy ones would come to our senses and stay off the streets, that was okay. We were still a community.'"

God calls some to action, others to support, and still others to pray. Be confident in your calling. Each will be doing what is "right" in His eyes if they obey His call!

Obedience

To obey is better than sacrifice, and to hearken than the fat of rams.

1 Samuel 15:22 KJV

If they obey and serve him, they will spend the rest of their days in prosperity and their years in contentment.

Job 36:11

He who has my commandments and keeps them, he it is who loves me; and he who loves me will be loved by my Father, and I will love him and manifest myself to him.

John 14:21 RSV

The world and all its wanting, wanting, wanting is on the way out—but whoever does what God wants is set for eternity.

1 John 2:17 THE MESSAGE

Chickens

Jack London's wonderful classic, *White Fang,* tells the story of an animal, half dog half wolf, as he survives his life in the wild and then learns to live among men.

White Fang was very fond of chickens and on one occasion raided a chicken-roost and killed fifty hens. His master scolded him and then took him into the chicken yard. When White Fang saw his favorite food walking around right in front of him he obeyed his natural impulse and lunged for a chicken. He was immediately checked by his master's voice. They stayed in the chicken yard for quite a while and every time White Fang made a move toward a chicken his master's voice would stop him. In this way he learned what his master wanted—he had learned to ignore the chickens.

Out of love and a desire to obey his master's will, White Fang overcame his natural, inborn desires. He may not have understood the reason, but he chose to bend his will to his master's.

Let the simplicity and purity of White Fang's love and devotion to his master help you realize that your life will always be full of "chickens." What you have to decide is, whom will you serve?

Patience

You need to keep on patiently doing God's will if you want him to do for you all that he has promised.
Hebrews 10:36 TLB

Is your life full of difficulties and temptations? Then be happy, for when the way is rough, your patience has a chance to grow. So let it grow, and don't try to squirm out of your problems. For when your patience is finally in full bloom, then you will be ready for anything, strong in character, full and complete.
James 1:2-4 TLB

For ye have need of patience, that, after ye have done the will of God, ye might receive the promise.
Hebrews 10:36 KJV

Finishing is better than starting! Patience is better than pride! Don't be quick-tempered—that is being a fool.
Ecclesiastes 7:8-9 TLB

Impatience

"Have you, perchance, found a diamond pendant? I feel certain I lost it last night in your theater," a woman phoned to ask the theater manager.

"Not that I know, madam," the manager said, "but let me ask some of my employees. Please hold the line for a minute while I make inquiry. If it hasn't been found, we certainly will make a diligent search for it."

Returning to the phone a few minutes later, the manager said, "I have good news for you! The diamond pendant has been found!"

There was no reply to his news however. "Hello! Hello!" he called into the phone, and then he heard the dial tone. The woman who made the inquiry about the lost diamond pendant had failed to wait for his answer. She had not given her name, and attempts to trace her call were unsuccessful. The pendant was eventually sold to raise money for the theater.

We are often like this woman when we make our requests to God. We fail to wait on the Lord, to hear His reply. Instead, we rush ahead impatiently, having no idea He has a great blessing to give us if only we'd slow down long enough to receive it!

Patience

Put on a heart of compassion, kindness, humility, gentleness and patience; bearing with one another, and forgiving each other, whoever has a complaint against anyone; just as the Lord forgave you, so also should you.

Colossians 3:12-13 NASB

Be humble and gentle. Be patient with each other, making allowance for each other's faults because of your love.

Ephesians 4:2 NLT

God is the one who makes us patient and cheerful. I pray that he will help you live at peace with each other, as you follow Christ.

Romans 15:5 CEV

We do not want you to become lazy, but to imitate those who through faith and patience inherit what has been promised.

Hebrews 6:12

Squeeze Please

According to a fable, a woman showed up one snowy morning at 5 a.m. at the home of an "examiner" of "suitable mother" candidates. After she was ushered in, she had to sit for three hours past her appointment time before she was interviewed. The first question given to her in the interview was, "Can you spell?"

"Yes," she said.

"Then spell, 'cook.'"

The woman responded, "C-O-O-K." The examiner than asked, "Do you know anything about numbers?"

The woman replied, "Yes, sir, some things."

The examiner said, "Please add two plus two."

The candidate replied, "Four."

"Fine," announced the examiner. "We'll be in touch."

At the board meeting of examiners held the next day, the examiner reported that the woman had all the qualifications to be a fine mother. He said, "First I tested her on self-denial, making her arrive at five in the morning on a snowy day. Then I tested her on patience. She waited three hours without complaint. Third, I tested her on temper, asking her questions a child could answer. She never showed indignation or anger. She'll make a fine mother." And all on the board agreed.

When you think you've run out of patience, remember how there's always a little more toothpaste in the toothpaste tube. You just have to squeeze a little harder!

Peace

Peace I leave with you; My peace I give to you;
not as the world gives, do I give to you.
John 14:27 NASB

I will lie down and sleep in peace, for you alone,
O LORD, make me dwell in safety.
Psalm 4:8

You give peace of mind to all who love your Law.
Nothing can make them fall.
Psalm 119:165 CEV

Thou wilt keep him in perfect peace, whose mind
is stayed on thee: because he trusteth in thee.
Isaiah 26:3 KJV

Help Me!

In an article written for *America* magazine entitled "Praying in a Time of Depression," Jane Redmont wrote:

"On a quick trip to New York for a consulting job, a week or two into the anti-depressant drug and feeling no relief, I fell into a seven-hour anxiety attack with recurring suicidal ideations. On the morning after my arrival I found I could not focus my attention; yet focus was crucial in the job I was contracted to do for twenty-four hours, as recorder and process observer at a conference of urban activists that was beginning later that day. I felt as if I were about to jump out of my skin—or throw myself under a truck.

"An hour away from the beginning of the conference, walking uptown on a noisy Manhattan street in the afternoon, I prayed . . . perhaps out loud, I am not sure. I said with all my strength, 'Jesus, I don't usually ask You for much, but I am asking You now, in the name of all those people whom You healed . . . *help me*.'

"Within an hour, I was calm again."

God is our high tower, a refuge in times of trouble. We can pray in the midst of anxiety and depression and God will fill us with His peace that passes understanding.

Peace

Therefore being justified by faith, we have peace with God through our Lord Jesus Christ.

Romans 5:1 KJV

The meek will inherit the land and enjoy great peace.

Psalm 37:11

You will live in joy and peace. The mountains and hills will burst into song, and the trees of the field will clap their hands!

Isaiah 55:12 NLT

Before you know it, a sense of God's wholeness, everything coming together for good, will come and settle you down. It's wonderful what happens when Christ displaces worry at the center of your life.

Philippians 4:7 THE MESSAGE

The Real Meaning of Peace

There once was a king who offered a prize to the artist who would paint the best picture of peace. Many artists tried. The king looked at all the pictures. But there were only two he really liked, and he had to choose between them.

One picture was of a calm lake. The lake was a perfect mirror for peaceful towering mountains all around it. The other picture had mountains, too. But these were rugged and bare. Above was an angry, raining, thundering sky. This did not look peaceful at all.

But when the king looked closely, he saw behind the waterfall a tiny bush growing in a crack in the rock. In the bush a mother bird had built her nest. There, in the midst of the rush of angry water, sat the mother bird on her nest—in perfect peace.

Which picture do you think won the prize? The king chose the second picture. Do you know why?

"Because," explained the king, "peace does not mean to be in a place where there is no noise, trouble, or hard work. Peace means to be in the midst of all those things and still be calm in your heart. That is the real meaning of peace."

Perseverance

Consider it pure joy, my brothers, whenever you face trials of many kinds, because you know that the testing of your faith develops perseverance. Perseverance must finish its work so that you may be mature and compete, not lacking anything.
James 1:2-4

May the Master take you by the hand and lead you along the path of God's love and Christ's endurance.
2 Thessalonians 3:5
THE MESSAGE

Love bears up under anything and everything that comes, is ever ready to believe the best of every person, its hopes are fadeless under all circumstances, and it endures everything [without weakening].
1 Corinthians 13:7 AMP

But if anyone suffers as a Christian, he is not to be ashamed, but is to glorify God in this name.
1 Peter 4:16 NASB

Pressed, but not Crushed

Bathyspheres are amazing inventions. Operating like a miniature submarine, they have been used to explore the ocean in places so deep the water pressure would crush a conventional submarine as easily as if it were an aluminum can. Bathyspheres compensate for the intense water pressure with plates of steel several inches thick. The steel keeps the water out, but it also makes a bathysphere very heavy and difficult to maneuver. The space inside is cramped, allowing for only one or two people to survey the ocean floor by looking through a tiny plate-glass window.

What divers invariably find at every depth of the ocean are fish and other sea creatures! Some of these creatures are quite small and appear to have fairly normal skin. They look flexible and supple as they swim through the inky waters. How can they live at these depths without steel plating? They compensate for the outside pressure through equal and opposite pressure on the inside.

Spiritual fortitude works in the same way. The more negative the circumstances around us, the more we need to allow God's power to work within us to exert an equal and opposite pressure from the inside. With God on the inside, we can persevere in any situation and no pressure on earth can crush us!

Perseverance

"My grace is sufficient for you, for my power is made perfect in weakness." Therefore I will boast all the more gladly about my weaknesses, so that Christ's power may rest on me.

2 Corinthians 12:9

We also glory in tribulations, knowing that tribulation produces perseverance; and perseverance, character; and character, hope. Now hope does not disappoint, because the love of God has been poured out in our hearts by the Holy Spirit who was given to us.

Romans 5:3-5 NKJV

You need to persevere so that when you have done the will of God, you will receive what he has promised.

Hebrews 10:36

The good soil represents honest, good-hearted people who hear God's message, cling to it, and steadily produce a huge harvest.

Luke 8:15 NLT

An Oath of Perseverance

1. I will never give up so long as I know I'm right.
2. I will believe that all things will work out for me if I hang on until the end.
3. I will be courageous and undismayed in the face of odds.
4. I will not permit anyone to intimidate me or deter me from my goals.
5. I will fight to overcome all physical limitations and setbacks.
6. I will try again and again and yet again to accomplish my dreams.
7. I will take new faith and resolution from the knowledge that all successful people have had to overcome defeat and adversity.
8. I will never surrender to discouragement or despair, no matter what.

Herman Sherman

Recite these vows every morning. Keep them with you and review them when you're stuck in traffic, trapped in a tense meeting, tossing and turning at night, preparing to meet a deadline, or sitting down for a serious talk with your child.

Prayer

If you believe, you will receive whatever you ask for in prayer.

Matthew 21:22

Don't quit in hard times; pray all the harder.

Romans 12:12 THE MESSAGE

The eyes of the Lord watch over those who do right, and his ears are open to their prayers.

1 Peter 3:12 NLT

He will respond to the prayer of the destitute; he will not despise their plea.

Psalm 102:17

The Red Umbrella

In a small farming community in the Midwest, the farmers didn't know what to do. The drought was dragging on and on for what seemed an eternity. The rain was very important to the community's way of life. As the problem became more urgent, the local church felt it was time to get involved and planned a prayer meeting in order to ask for rain.

When the pastor arrived, he watched as his congregation continued to file in. He slowly circulated from group to group as he made his way to the front in order to officially begin the meeting. As the pastor finally secured his place in front of his flock, his thoughts were on the importance of quieting the crowd and starting the meeting.

Just as he began asking for quiet, he noticed an eleven-year-old girl sitting in the front row. She was angelically beaming with excitement and laying next to her was her bright red umbrella, poised for use.

The beauty and innocence of this sight made the pastor smile to himself as he realized the faith this young girl possessed that the rest of the people in the room seemed to have forgotten. For the rest had come just to pray for rain—she had come to see God answer.

Prayer

The LORD has heard my cry for mercy; the LORD accepts my prayer.

Psalm 6:9

Pray at all times and on every occasion in the power of the Holy Spirit. Stay alert and be persistent in your prayers for all Christians everywhere.

Ephesians 6:18 NLT

In the morning, O LORD, you hear my voice; in the morning I lay my requests before you and wait in expectation.

Psalm 5:3

Pray diligently. Stay alert, with your eyes wide open in gratitude.

Colossians 4:2 THE MESSAGE

Innocent Petitions

In her book, *Mothering by Heart,* Robin
Jones Gunn tells how she learned everything she
needed to know about prayer in the second grade.
Her family had moved from Reno to Portland just
a few days before her daughter Rachel's first day
of second grade. In Reno, Rachel had a best friend
named Kristin. The night before her first day of
school, Rachel prayed that God would send her a
new best friend and that her name would be Kristin.

Robin tried to think of a way to explain to
her daughter that prayer doesn't work that way.
She hoped that Rachel's innocent faith wouldn't
be hurt. The next day, when they got to the
classroom, Rachel found her name on her desk
and Robin sat down at the desk next to Rachel's.
She was just about to explain to Rachel that she
should accept whatever new friends God brought
to her, when she saw something out of the corner
of her eye. The name on the desk next to Rachel's
read: "Kristin." And when Kristin walked in and
took her seat, Robin saw that she had brown hair,
just like the Kristin in Reno.

God loves it when we come to Him with
that kind of childlike faith.

Priorities

Seek the LORD and his strength, seek his presence continually! Remember the wonderful works that he has done, the wonders he wrought, the judgments he uttered.

1 Chronicles 16:11-12 RSV

Let the word of Christ dwell in you richly in all wisdom; teaching and admonishing one another in psalms and hymns and spiritual songs, singing with grace in your hearts to the Lord. And whatsoever ye do in word or deed, do all in the name of the Lord Jesus, giving thanks to God and the Father by him.

Colossians 3:16-17 KJV

God, my God! How I search for you! How I thirst for you in this parched and weary land where there is no water. How I long to find you! At last I shall be fully satisfied; I will praise you with great joy.

Psalm 63:1,5 TLB

What good will it be for a man if he gains the whole world, yet forfeits his soul?

Matthew 16:26

The Gift of Life

Once a nationally syndicated columnist and now an author, Anna Quindlen seems to have enjoyed success at everything she has attempted. However, in taking a fellow commentator to task after he made light of teenage problems, Anna was reminded of the two attempts she had made to end her own life at age sixteen. She writes, "I was really driven through my high school years. I always had to be perfect in every way, ranging from how I looked to how my grades were. It was too much pressure."

In the early 1970s, Anna's mother died from ovarian cancer. This tragedy cured Anna from any desire to commit suicide. Her attitude toward life changed. "I could never look at life as anything but a great gift. I realized I didn't have any business taking it for granted."

When we are faced with the realization that life is temporary, we can finally come to grips with what is important. When we face our own immortality, our priorities quickly come into focus.

Consider your life as God's gift to you. Every moment is precious, so cherish them all. In doing so, you'll find purpose and meaning for each day.

Priorities

If any man will come after me, let him deny himself, and take up his cross daily, and follow me. For whosoever will save his life shall lose it: but whosoever will lose his life for my sake, the same shall save it. For what is a man advantaged, if he gain the whole world, and lose himself, or be cast away?

Luke 9:23-25 KJV

Speak to one another with psalms, hymns and spiritual songs. Sing and make music in your heart to the Lord, always giving thanks to God the Father for everything, in the name of our Lord Jesus Christ.

Ephesians 5:19-20

With Jesus' help, let us continually offer our sacrifice of praise to God by proclaiming the glory of his name.

Hebrews 13:15 NLT

I appeal to you therefore, brethren, by the mercies of God, to present your bodies as a living sacrifice, holy and acceptable to God, which is your spiritual worship.

Romans 12:1 RSV

To My Grown-up Son

My hands were busy through the day;
I didn't have much time to play
The little games you asked me to—
I didn't have much time for you.
I'd wash your clothes, I'd sew and cook;
But when you'd bring your picture book
And ask me please to share your fun,
I'd say: "A little later, son."

I'd tuck you in all safe at night,
And hear your prayers, turn out the light,
Then tiptoe softly to the door. . . .
I wish I'd stayed a minute more.

For life is short, the years rush past. . . .
A little boy grows up so fast.
No longer is he at your side,
His precious secrets to confide.
The picture books are put away;
There are no longer games to play.
No good-night kiss, no prayers to hear—
That all belongs to yesteryear.

My hands, once busy, now are still.
The days are long and hard to fill.
I wish I could go back and do
The little things you asked me to.

Anonymous

Protection

If you make the Most High your dwelling—even the LORD, who is my refuge—then no harm will befall you, no disaster will come near your tent. For he will command his angels concerning you to guard you in all your ways; they will lift you up in their hands, so that you will not strike your foot against a stone.

Psalm 91:9-12

No weapon forged against you will prevail, and you will refute every tongue that accuses you. This is the heritage of the servants of the LORD, and this is their vindication from me.

Isaiah 54:17

In peace I will both lie down and sleep; for thou alone, O LORD, makest me dwell in safety.

Psalm 4:8 RSV

The LORD will keep you from all harm—he will watch over your life; the LORD will watch over your coming and going both now and forevermore.

Psalm 121:7-8

A Real Traffic-stopper

While driving along the freeway, the adults in the front seat of a car were talking when suddenly, they heard the horrifying sound of a car door opening, the whistle of wind, and a sickening thud. They quickly turned and saw that the three-year-old child riding in the back seat had fallen out of the car and was tumbling along the freeway. The driver screeched to a stop, and then raced back toward her child. To her surprise, she found that all the traffic had stopped just a few feet away from her child. Her daughter had not been hit.

A truck driver drove the girl to a nearby hospital. The doctors there rushed her into the emergency room, and soon came back with the good news: Other than a few scrapes and bruises, the girl was fine; no broken bones, no apparent internal damage.

As the mother rushed to her child, the little girl opened her eyes and said, "Mommy, you know I wasn't afraid. While I was lying on the road waiting for you to get back to me, I looked up and right there I saw Jesus holding back the traffic with His arms out."

God truly watches over us with loving care.

Protection

The LORD shall preserve you from all evil; He shall preserve your soul. The LORD shall preserve your going out and your coming in from this time forth, and even forevermore.

Psalm 121:7-8 NKJV

When you pass through the waters, I will be with you; and when you pass through the rivers, they will not sweep over you. When you walk through the fire, you will not be burned; the flames will not set you ablaze.

Isaiah 43:2

GOD's angel sets up a circle of protection around us while we pray.

Psalm 34:7 THE MESSAGE

The name of the LORD is a strong fortress; the godly run to him and are safe.

Proverbs 18:10 NLT

God Sees You

During the terrible days of the Blitz in
World War II, a father—holding his young
daughter by the hand—ran from a building that
had been struck by a bomb. Several days before, a
shell explosion had left a large hole in the front
yard. Seeking shelter as quickly as possible, the
father jumped into the hole and then held up his
arms for his young daughter to follow.

Terrified by the explosions around her, but
unable to see her father in the shadow of the hole,
she cried, "I can't see you, Papa!"

The father looked up against the sky, lit
with white tracer lights and tinted red by burning
buildings and called to his daughter, who was
standing at the hole's edge, "But I can see you,
my darling. Jump!"

The little girl jumped—not because she
could see her father, but because he could see her.
She trusted him to tell her the truth and to do
what was best for her.

We may not be able to clearly discern where
our Heavenly Father is leading us, but we can
trust that He is protecting us every step of the
way. He has promised that when we turn to Him,
we will be safe.

Reconciliation

Pursue peace with all people, and holiness, without which no one will see the Lord: looking carefully lest anyone fall short of the grace of God; lest any root of bitterness springing up cause trouble, and by this many become defiled.

Hebrews 12:14-15 NKJV

Blessed are the merciful: for they shall obtain mercy.

Matthew 5:7 KJV

Do not be overcome by evil, but overcome evil with good.

Romans 12:21

Be kind to each other, tenderhearted, forgiving one another, just as God through Christ has forgiven you.

Ephesians 4:32 NLT

Warm Reconciliation

Years after her experience in a Nazi concentration camp, Corrie ten Boom found herself standing face to face with one of the most cruel and heartless German guards she had met while in the camp. This man had humiliated and degraded both her and her sister.

Now he stood before her with an outstretched hand, asking, "Will you forgive me?" Corrie said, "I stood there with coldness clutching at my heart, but I know that the will can function regardless of the temperature of the heart. I prayed, 'Jesus, help me!' Woodenly, mechanically I thrust my hand into the one stretched out to me and I experienced an incredible thing. The current started in my shoulder, raced down into my arm, and sprang into our clutched hands. Then this warm reconciliation seemed to flood my whole being, bringing tears to my eyes. 'I forgive you, brother,' I cried with my whole heart. For a long moment we grasped each other's hands, the former guard, the former prisoner. I have never known the love of God so intensely as I did in that moment!"

We learn the true meaning of mercy when it is given to us undeserved; and when we choose to extend mercy to others, God is faithful to soften our hearts with His great love and mercy. We are freed when we free another.

Reconciliation

The discretion of a man makes him slow to anger,
and his glory is to overlook a transgression.
Proverbs 19:11 NKJV

Do not resist an evil person. If someone strikes
you on the right cheek, turn to him the other also.
Matthew 5:39

And whenever you stand praying, forgive, if you
have anything against any one; so that your Father
also who is in heaven may forgive you your trespasses.
Mark 11:25 RSV

If thy brother trespass against thee, rebuke him;
and if he repent, forgive him.
Luke 17:3 KJV

Silence Beyond Words

Marie Louise de La Ramee says in *Ouida,* "There are many moments in friendship, as in love, when silence is beyond words. The faults of our friend may be clear to us, but it is well to seem to shut our eyes to them.

"Friendship is usually treated by the majority of mankind as a tough and everlasting thing which will survive all manner of bad treatment. But this is an exceedingly great and foolish error; it may die in an hour of a single unwise word."

If the words "I love you" are the most important three words in a marriage, the words "I'm sorry" are probably the *two* most important! The more a spouse is willing to admit fault, the greater the likelihood the other spouse will also grow to be vulnerable enough to admit error. That doesn't mean a person should apologize for an error that has not been made; to do so would be to become a doormat or to manifest a false humility. When one is standing in the right, although the other cannot see it, the better approach is silence. Not saying, "I'm not speaking to you until you apologize," but saying nothing more about the issue. Remember, sometimes silence is indeed golden.

Rejection

You have been my helper. Do not reject me or forsake me, O God my Savior. Though my father and mother forsake me, the LORD will receive me.

Psalm 27:9-10

[Jesus said:] "Those the Father has given me will come to me, and I will never reject them."

John 6:37 NLT

Everyone who honors your name can trust you, because you are faithful to all who depend on you.

Psalm 9:10 CEV

He who rejects this instruction does not reject man but God, who gives you his Holy Spirit.

1 Thessalonians 4:8

Turning Rejection into Opportunity

Sharen was just out of school, eager to start her newspaper career, but kept encountering rejection because of the age-old dilemma—she couldn't get a job because she lacked experience, and she couldn't get experience without a job.

She saw a classified ad for a position, which said applicants would be interviewed at 10 a.m. the next day. She worked all night to make her resume look as promising as possible, and prepared a portfolio of her writing samples.

Arriving early the next morning, she was stunned to see a long line. As she took her place at the end of the line, she recognized several competitors as older, more experienced reporters.

Sharen had an idea. She wrote a note, and took it to the editor's secretary, telling her it was extremely important to show it to her boss immediately.

When the editor read the note, he hurried through the rest of the interviews. It said, "Dear Sir, I'm the young woman who is tenth in line. Please don't make any decisions until you see me."

This kind of resourcefulness and refusal to take no for an answer was just what the editor was looking for in a reporter. Sharen had turned rejection into opportunity.

Rejection

Behold what manner of love the Father has bestowed on us, that we should be called children of God! Therefore the world does not know us, because it did not know Him.

1 John 3:1 NKJV

A man of many companions may come to ruin, but there is a friend who sticks closer than a brother.

Proverbs 18:24

Long ago, even before he made the world, God loved and chose us in Christ to be holy and without fault in his eyes.

Ephesians 1:4 NLT

For the Lord will not forsake his people; he will not abandon his heritage; for justice will return to the righteous, and all the upright in heart will follow it.

Psalm 94:14-15 RSV

Overcoming Rejection

John Hull, author of *Touching the Rock,* is blind. In telling his life story, he recounts that his mother spent two years attending Melbourne High School, lodging there with Mildred Treloar. While living with her, John's mother began attending weekly Bible classes with her. Over the months, her personal dedication to the Lord was renewed and deepened as the pages of the Bible came alive for her. It was this vibrant faith that she passed to her son, John.

Where did Mildred Treloar acquire her faith? From her father. Mr. Treloar had desired to become a minister as a young man, but was rejected by his denomination. Rather than become bitter, he poured his faith into Mildred. While she lived with Mildred, John's mother spent many hours reading the Bible to Mr. Treloar, and vividly recalled for him his great hope of heaven. Why was Mr. Treloar considered to be unacceptable as a minister? He was blind!

If Mr. Treloar had given in to bitterness or self-pity when his denomination rejected him, he could not have passed his vibrant faith on to his daughter. When we're rejected, we can overcome it by turning to God, instead of away from Him. He will never reject us!

Relationships

But if we walk in the light, as he is in the light, we have fellowship with one another, and the blood of Jesus, his Son, purifies us from all sin.

1 John 1:7

And the Scripture was fulfilled which says, "Abraham believed God, and it was accounted to him for righteousness." And he was called the friend of God.

James 2:23 NKJV

Now I tell you to love each other, as I have loved you. The greatest way to show love for friends is to die for them. And you are my friends, if you obey me.

John 15:12-14 CEV

Friends love through all kinds of weather, and families stick together in all kinds of trouble.

Proverbs 17:17 THE MESSAGE

Wars and Rumors of Wars

A little girl once asked her father how wars got started.

"Well," said her father, "suppose America persisted in quarreling with England, and . . ."

"But," interrupted her mother, "America must never quarrel with England."

"I know," said the father, "but I am only using a hypothetical instance."

"But you are misleading the child," protested Mom.

"No, I am not," replied the father indignantly, with an edge of anger in his tone.

"Never mind, Daddy," the little girl interjected, "I think I know how wars get started."

Most major arguments don't begin major, but are rooted in a small annoyances, breaches, or trespasses. It's like the mighty oak that stood on the skyline of the Rocky Mountains. The tree had survived hail, heavy snows, bitter cold, and ferocious storms for more than a century. It was finally felled not by a great lightning strike or an avalanche, but by an attack of tiny beetles.

A little hurt, neglect, or insult can be the beginning of the end for virtually any relationship. Therefore, take care what you say, check your attitude, and be quick to ask for forgiveness when you've been wrong. Maintain those important relationships in your life and don't let the "tiny beetles" eat away at them.

Relationships

But who am I and who are my people that we should be able to offer as generously as this? For all things come from Thee, and from Thy hand we have given Thee.

1 Chronicles 29:14 NASB

Jesus went over to the collection box in the Temple and sat and watched as the crowds dropped in their money. Many rich people put in large amounts. Then a poor widow came and dropped in two pennies. He called his disciples to him and said, "I assure you, this poor widow has given more than all the others have given. For they gave a tiny part of their surplus, but she, poor as she is, has given everything she has."

Mark 12:41-44 NLT

God did not keep back his own Son, but he gave him for us. If God did this, won't he freely give us everything else?

Romans 8:32 CEV

If I give all I possess to the poor and surrender my body to the flames, but have not love, I gain nothing.

1 Corinthians 13:3

A Generous Spirit
Can Change Your World

Gale was a shy, quiet little girl. One day she came home and told her parents she wanted to make a valentine for everyone in her class. That night her dad and mom talked about it. Gale wasn't very popular. The other kids didn't include her in their games. She always walked home by herself. What if she went to all the trouble and then didn't receive any valentines?

They decided to encourage her anyway. For three weeks, for hours after school, Gale worked until she had made 35 valentines.

Valentine's Day dawned, and Gale excitedly put her handiwork into a paper bag and bolted out the door. Trying to be prepared for her disappointment, Gale's parents had plans to take her out for ice cream that night.

That afternoon, Gale came running home, all out of breath. Her arms were empty. Her folks expected her to burst into tears. "Not a one, not a one," Gale said, over and over. Her mom and dad looked at her and held each other.

Then she added, "I didn't forget a single kid."

One of the beautiful benefits of being generous toward others is that it's so rewarding it changes the way we look at the world.

Renewal

Therefore if any man be in Christ, he is a new creature: old things are passed away; behold, all things are become new.

2 Corinthians 5:17 KJV

Be made new in the attitude of your minds; and to put on the new self, created to be like God in true righteousness and holiness.

Ephesians 4:23-24

My friends, I don't feel that I have already arrived. But I forget what is behind, and I struggle for what is ahead. I run toward the goal, so that I can win the prize of being called to heaven.

Philippians 3:13-14 CEV

Do not lie to one another, since you have put off the old man with his deeds, and have put on the new man who is renewed in knowledge according to the image of Him who created him.

Colossians 3:9-10 NKJV

Rescue Me

Can the Lord speak through a pop song? Fontella Bass thinks so. During 1990, she was at the lowest point in her life. It had been twenty-five years since her rhythm-and-blues single had hit number one on the charts. She had no career to speak of, and she was broke, tired, and cold. The only heat in her tiny house came from a gas stove in the kitchen. She had also strayed far from the church where she had started singing gospel songs as a child.

Fontella says, "I said a long prayer. I said, 'I need to see a sign to continue on.'" No sooner had she prayed than she heard her hit song, "Rescue Me," on a television commercial! To her, it was as if "the Lord had stepped right into my world!"

Fontella was unaware that American Express had been using her song as part of a commercial. Officials had been unable to locate her to pay her royalties. Not only did she receive back-royalties, but new opportunities for her to sing began to open.

When we cry out to God because we've realized the futility of our own efforts, He renews our hope and brings us blessings far greater than we could have imagined.

Renewal

Restore to me the joy of thy salvation, and uphold me with a willing spirit. The sacrifice acceptable to God is a broken spirit; a broken and contrite heart, O God, thou wilt not despise.

Psalm 51:12,17 RSV

Our God, make us strong again! Smile on us and save us.

Psalm 80:3 CEV

Turn us back to You, O LORD, and we will be restored; renew our days as of old.

Lamentations 5:21 NKJV

And the God of all grace, who called you to his eternal glory in Christ, after you have suffered a little while, will himself restore you and make you strong, firm and steadfast.

1 Peter 5:10

This Old Heart

At a crucial transition time in her life, a Christian woman cried out to the Lord, despairing over the lack of spiritual power she was experiencing in her life. Suddenly she sensed Jesus standing beside her, asking, "May I have the keys to your life?"

The experience was so realistic, the woman reached into her pocket and took out a ring of keys. "Are all the keys here?" the Lord asked.

"Yes, except the key to one small room in my life."

"If you cannot trust Me in all rooms of your life, I cannot accept any of the keys."

The woman was so overwhelmed at the thought of the Lord moving out of her life altogether, she cried, "Lord! Take the keys to all the rooms of my life!"

Many of us have rooms we hope no one will ever see. We intend to clean them out someday, but someday never seems to come. When we invite Jesus into these rooms, He will clean them and restore them. With Him, we have the courage to throw away all the junk, and He will fill the rooms with His love and peace and joy. His grace beautifies the rooms, and He makes Himself at home there.

Stewardship

And he sat down opposite the treasury, and watched the multitude putting money into the treasury. Many rich people put in large sums. And a poor widow came, and put in two copper coins, which make a penny. And he called his disciples to him, and said to them, "Truly, I say to you, this poor widow has put in more than all those who are contributing to the treasury."

Mark 12:41-43 RSV

Command those who are rich in this present world not to be arrogant nor to put their hope in wealth, which is so uncertain, but to put their hope in God, who richly provides us with everything for our enjoyment. Command them to do good, to be rich in good deeds, and to be generous and willing to share.

1 Timothy 6:17-18

Although they were going through hard times and were very poor, they were glad to give generously. They gave as much as they could afford and even more, simply because they wanted to.

2 Corinthians 8:2-3 CEV

On every Lord's Day, each of you should put aside some amount of money in relation to what you have earned and save it for this offering. Don't wait until I get there and then try to collect it all at once.

1 Corinthians 16:2 NLT

Turning Pennies into Fortunes

Some years ago in Philadelphia, fifty-seven pennies were found under a little girl's pillow, pennies that left an unforgettable mark on the city.

The little girl attended what was called the Temple Sunday School. She, like many other children, joined their parents in supporting the expansion of the facilities by saving their pennies. Two years after she started her savings, the little girl became ill and died. Shortly after her death, her parents found a small purse under her pillow, with fifty-seven pennies and a piece of paper with the following delicately handwritten note: "To help build the Temple bigger, so more children can go to Sunday School."

The pastor told the story to the congregation, and the local newspaper featured it, and soon her story had spread across the country. Soon the pennies grew into dollars, and the dollars into a huge fortune.

The outcome can be seen in Philadelphia today, where there is a church that will seat 3,000 persons; Temple University, home to thousands of students, including famous alumnus Bill Cosby; Temple Hospital; and, yes, Temple Sunday School.

This is how stewardship works: Because one little girl gave what she could, millions were inspired to "go and do likewise."

Stewardship

The Lord answered, "Who then is the faithful and wise manager, whom the master puts in charge of his servants to give them their food allowance at the proper time? It will be good for that servant whom the master finds doing so when he returns."

Luke 12:42-43

Now, a person who is put in charge as a manager must be faithful.

1 Corinthians 4:2 NLT

Each of you has been blessed with one of God's many wonderful gifts to be used in the service of others. So use your gift well.

1 Peter 4:10 CEV

Good will come to him who is generous and lends freely, who conducts his affairs with justice.

Psalm 112:5

Stewardship Starts in the Heart

Here's how Oseola McCarty learned to practice stewardship.

She spent most of her life helping people look nice.

You see, she took in bundles of dirty clothes, and washed and ironed them. She started after having to drop out of school in the sixth grade and carried out her work into her eighties.

Oseola never married, never had children. And for most of her eighty-seven years, Oseola McCarty spent almost no money. She lived in her old family home and wore simple clothes. She saved her money, most of it dollar bills and change, until she had amassed a little over $150,000.

Then she made what people in Hattiesburg, Mississippi, are calling "The Gift." She donated her entire savings—all $150,000—to black college students across the state.

"I know it won't be too many years before I pass on," she explained, "and I wanted to share my wealth with the children."

Before her death, she was able to witness a number of "her children" graduate with the help of her financial support.

She teaches us all that stewardship starts in the heart, and when our hearts are full of love and gratitude, we'll find a way to leave a legacy.

Strength

I will love thee, O Lord, my strength.

Psalm 18:1 KJV

The Lord will give strength to His people; the Lord will bless His people with peace.

Psalm 29:11 NASB

God is wonderful and glorious. I pray that his Spirit will make you become strong followers and that Christ will live in your hearts because of your faith. Stand firm and be deeply rooted in his love.

Ephesians 3:16-17 CEV

I can do everything through him who gives me strength.

Philippians 4:13

Where True Strength Comes From

A house is just a house, until love comes in, transforming ordinary dust into angel dust.

Money has the power to pay for a house, but only love can furnish it with homey feelings.

Duty can make you pack a kid's lunch, but love inspires you to tuck a little note inside.

Keeping up can cause you to own a TV set, but love controls the remote.

Needing time alone can lead you to put the children to bed, but love tucks the covers in and reads a story.

Obligation can make you buy groceries, but love enhances a delicious meal with flowers and candles.

Compulsion keeps a sparkling house and manicured lawn, but love creates a play place inside and out.

Responsibility carries out the necessary tasks, but love enables you to do them for the sheer joy of service.

Accountability can motivate you to pay the bills, but love inspires you to offer a prayer of thanks for blessings symbolized by each check.

Duty can motivate you to call your faraway family members, but love frees you to prepare a care package full of their favorite things.

Yes, strength of will can keep things from falling into disrepair, but the power of love makes life worth living.

Strength

The LORD is my strength and my song; he has become my salvation.

Psalm 118:14

Behold, God is my salvation; I will trust, and will not be afraid; for the Lord God is my strength and my song, and he has become my salvation.

Isaiah 12:2 RSV

Sing aloud to God our strength; make a joyful shout to the God of Jacob.

Psalm 81:1 NKJV

My body and mind may fail, but you are my strength and my choice forever.

Psalm 73:26 CEV

Our Refuge and Strength

Norma Zimmer had a difficult childhood as a result of her parents' drinking. Singing was her way to escape. As a high school senior, Norma was invited to be a featured soloist at the University Christian Church in Seattle. When her parents heard she was going to sing, they both insisted on attending the service. She says about that morning, "I stole glances at the congregation, trying to find my parents . . . then in horror I saw them—weaving down the aisle. They were late. The congregation stared. I don't know how I ever got through that morning."

After she sang and took her seat, her heart pounding, the pastor preached: "God is our refuge and strength, a tested help in time of trouble."

She says, "My own trouble seemed to bear down on me with tremendous weight. . . . I realized how desperate life in our family was without God. . . . Jesus came into my life not only as Savior but for daily strength and direction."

The salvation God offers us is not only for our future benefit, but for our day-to-day needs in the present. He is an ever-present help in times of trouble. Daily rely on Him for peace and direction— He *is* your refuge and your strength.

Stress

Consider the blameless, observe the upright; there is a future for the man of peace.

Psalm 37:37

And the peace of God, which passeth all understanding, shall keep your hearts and minds through Christ Jesus.

Philippians 4:7 KJV

Come to Me, all you who labor and are heavy laden, and I will give you rest.

Matthew 11:28 NKJV

I tell you to love your enemies and pray for anyone who mistreats you.

Matthew 5:44 CEV

Love Lasers

Claire Townsend worked in one of our country's most stressful workplaces—a major motion picture studio. She came to dread the daily morning meetings. New owners had taken control of the studio, jobs were uncertain, and teamwork disappeared.

As she struggled with her stress, Claire paid more attention to her spiritual life. She began to pray again, and rediscovered the power of God's love. Even so, the morning meetings exhausted her.

Then during a particularly tense meeting, a thought came to her: *Pray, pray, pray. Do it now.* As she did so she felt God's love pulsating within her, then radiating out like sunlight. She aimed a "love laser" toward the person who was making her feel the worst. This coworker suddenly got quiet, eyed her curiously, and Claire smiled back. One by one, she beamed God's love to each person around the table as she silently prayed.

Within minutes, the tone of the meeting completely changed. Compromise replaced confrontation. As the group relaxed, they became more creative and effective. From that day on, Claire looked forward to the meetings as an opportunity to share God's love.

Nobody else needs to know if you pray to reduce stress next time you're in a tension-filled group, but you'll know, and God will know.

Stress

Be anxious for nothing, but in everything by prayer and supplication, with thanksgiving, let your requests be made known to God; and the peace of God, which surpasses all understanding, will guard your hearts and minds through Christ Jesus.

Philippians 4:6-7 NKJV

But when I am afraid, I will put my confidence in you. Yes, I will trust the promises of God. And since I am trusting him, what can mere man do to me?

Psalm 56:3-4 TLB

Be not afraid of sudden fear, neither of the desolation of the wicked, when it cometh. For the LORD shall be thy confidence, and shall keep thy foot from being taken.

Proverbs 3:25-26 KJV

Even though I walk through the valley of the shadow of death, I will fear no evil, for you are with me; your rod and your staff, they comfort me.

Psalm 23:4

Calm and Collected

During the four-week siege of Tientsin, in June of 1900, Herbert Hoover helped erect barricades around the foreign compound and organized all the able-bodied men into a protective force to man them. Mrs. Hoover went to work, too—helping set up a hospital, taking her turn nursing the wounded, and serving tea every afternoon to those on sentry duty.

One afternoon, while she was sitting at home playing solitaire, a shell suddenly burst nearby, leaving a big hole in the backyard. A little later a second shell hit the road in front of the house. Then came a third shell. This one burst through one of the windows of the house and demolished a post by the staircase.

Several reporters covering the siege rushed into the living room to see if she was all right and found her sitting at the card table. "I don't seem to be winning this hand," she remarked coolly, "but that was the third shell and therefore the last one for the present anyway. Their pattern is three in a row. Let's go and have tea."

Staying calm in the face of danger is your best defense. Worrying about what *might* happen causes unnecessary stress. So relax, and remember you're in God's hands.

Success

People should eat and drink and enjoy the fruits of their labor, for these are gifts from God.

Ecclesiastes 3:13 NLT

Wealth and riches are in his house, and his righteousness endures forever.

Psalm 112:3

The LORD your God will make you abound in all the work of your hand, in the fruit of your body, in the increase of your livestock, and in the produce of your land for good.

Deuteronomy 30:9 NKJV

They are like trees growing beside a stream, trees that produce fruit in season and always have leaves. Those people succeed in everything they do.

Psalm 1:3 CEV

True Success

Jenny Lind was known as "The Swedish Nightingale" during her very successful career as an operatic singer. She became one of the wealthiest artists of her time, yet she left the stage at her peak and never returned.

Countless people speculated as to the reason for her leaving, and most people wondered how she could give up so much applause, fame, and money. However, she was content to live in privacy in a home by the sea.

One day a friend found her on the beach, her Bible on her knees, looking out into the glorious glow of a sunset. As they talked, the friend asked, "Madame, how is it that you ever came to abandon the stage at the height of your success?"

She answered quietly, "When every day it made me think less of this (laying a finger on her Bible) and nothing at all of that (pointing to the sunset), what else could I do?"

The world may never understand your decision to follow God's way. But then, perhaps God cannot understand a decision to pursue what the world offers when He has such great rewards in store for those who follow Him. True success is found in knowing and loving God.

Success

True humility and respect for the Lord lead a man to riches, honor and long life.

Proverbs 22:4 TLB

And it is a good thing to receive wealth from God and the good health to enjoy it. To enjoy your work and accept your lot in life—that is indeed a gift from God.

Ecclesiastes 5:19 NLT

You will decide on a matter, and it will be established for you, and light will shine on your ways.

Job 22:28 RSV

Wealth and Glory accompany me—also substantial Honor and a Good Name. My benefits are worth more than a big salary, even a very big salary; the returns on me exceed any imaginable bonus.

Proverbs 8:18-19
THE MESSAGE

You Mustn't Quit

When things go wrong, as they sometimes will,
When the road you're trudging seems all uphill,
When the funds are low and the debts are high
And you want to smile, but you have to sigh,
When care is pressing you down a bit,
Rest! If you must—but never quit.
Life is queer, with its twists and turns,
As every one of us sometimes learns,
And many a failure turns about
When he might have won if he'd stuck it out;
Stick to your task, though the pace seems slow —
You may succeed with one more blow.
Success is failure turned inside out—
The silver tint of the clouds of doubt—
And you never can tell how close you are,
It may be near when it seems afar;
So stick to the fight when you're hardest hit—
It's when things seem worst that
YOU MUSTN'T QUIT.

—Anonymous

If you quit today, you'll never know what
lies just around the bend.

Suffering

He is despised and rejected by men, a Man of sorrows and acquainted with grief. And we hid, as it were, our faces from Him; He was despised, and we did not esteem Him.

Isaiah 53:3 NKJV

He then began to teach them that the Son of Man must suffer many things and be rejected by the elders, chief priests and teachers of the law, and that he must be killed and after three days rise again.

Mark 8:31

For as the sufferings of Christ abound in us, so our consolation also aboundeth by Christ.

2 Corinthians 1:5 KJV

I am sure that what we are suffering now cannot compare with the glory that will be shown to us.

Romans 8:18 CEV

Peace in the Midst of Suffering

A minister once went to the hospital to visit a friend named Ruth. She and her husband had served as missionaries for more than twenty years. It seemed incongruous that this woman should now be suffering in the final stages of inoperable lung cancer. She had never smoked. Rounds of agonizing chemotherapy had taken their toll and now even that treatment had been abandoned. Ruth was left to wait for inevitable death. The minister quickly prayed about what he might say to her.

Other than her loss of hair, Ruth showed no signs of advanced cancer. She radiated peace as she began to tell the minister how thankful she was that God had allowed her to walk down this path of suffering. "I've always been a Martha," she said, "too busy to sit at the feet of Jesus, but God has used this cancer to slow me down so that I can get to know Him in ways I never did before." The minister left her room encouraged, not downcast. He had been asking God why Ruth had to suffer. Meanwhile, Ruth was thanking Him in the midst of the experience!

God never causes our suffering, but when we look to Him in the midst of it, He can use it for our good.

Suffering

I delight in weaknesses, in insults, in hardships, in persecutions, in difficulties. For when I am weak, then I am strong.

2 Corinthians 12:10

Thou therefore endure hardness, as a good soldier of Jesus Christ.

2 Timothy 2:3 KJV

For to you it has been granted on behalf of Christ, not only to believe in Him, but also to suffer for His sake.

Philippians 1:29 NKJV

Cast thy burden upon the LORD, and he shall sustain thee: he shall never suffer the righteous to be moved.

Psalm 55:22 KJV

Suffering Leads to Joy

In her book *The Spirituality of Gentleness*, Judith Lechman speaks of suffering and the spiritual benefits it can produce in a life.

"Bearing crosses can be a bitter thing indeed, if we grow afraid of letting go. Years ago I copied a striking phrase in my journal: 'and I rejoice over the falling leaves of self.' . . . It has been a reminder to me over the years that with suffering comes joy.

"If we turn back to God and ask for His strength to renounce, not our suffering, not our pain, not a particular cross, but the tight hold we have on the leaves of self, as we let go of them and begin to 'live for the sake of Jesus Christ,' our suffering merges with His. In this sharing, we begin to know the terrible sacrifice that Christ made for us.

"Ever so slowly, our bitterness fades as we finally grasp that 'He suffered, and was a Sacrifice, to make our sufferings and sacrifice of ourselves fit to be received by God.' In a process that I can only describe as mysterious, placing our life completely in God's hands as we bear the crosses He gives us becomes an act of adoration and praise that takes us beyond suffering to joy."

Temptation

Put on the whole armor of God, that you may be able to stand against the wiles of the devil.

Ephesians 6:11 NKJV

Be self-controlled and alert. Your enemy the devil prowls around like a roaring lion looking for someone to devour.

1 Peter 5:8

So you see, the Lord knows how to rescue godly people from their trials, even while punishing the wicked right up until the day of judgment.

2 Peter 2:9 NLT

Stay alert, be in prayer, so you don't enter the danger zone without even knowing it. Don't be naive. Part of you is eager, ready for anything in God; but another part is as lazy as an old dog sleeping by the fire.

Mark 14:38 THE MESSAGE

A Needed Adjustment

A woman was working on her taxes one night when she made an unpleasant discovery. She noticed that her income from the previous year was higher than she had thought, so she owed more taxes than she had anticipated. Her son suggested she just "adjust" the figures. "I can't do that," she replied. "That would be lying."

Yet even as she spoke, the woman realized that she had already given in to the same temptation at work. At the bank where she worked, her boss had often asked her to change dates, add signatures, or "adjust" figures. That night she realized she could no longer participate in the deceit.

The next time her boss asked her to "help out," she refused. A few weeks later, the vice president of the bank asked the woman if she had altered any documents. She admitted that she had and was then told that others in the organization had been put in the same position. She and several other employees met with the board of directors, the truth came out, and her boss was fired.

Nobody can rob you of your integrity. You alone have the power to diminish or destroy it by the way you handle temptation.

Temptation

No temptation has overtaken you that is not common to man. God is faithful, and he will not let you be tempted beyond your strength, but with the temptation will also provide the way of escape, that you may be able to endure it.

1 Corinthians 10:13 RSV

For since he himself has now been through suffering and temptation, he knows what it is like when we suffer and are tempted, and he is wonderfully able to help us.

Hebrews 2:18 TLB

You are of God, little children, and have overcome them, because He who is in you is greater than he who is in the world.

1 John 4:4 NKJV

And lead us not into temptation, but deliver us from evil: For thine is the kingdom, and the power, and the glory, for ever. Amen.

Matthew 6:13 KJV

The Advocate

Charles H. Spurgeon sometimes stopped in his pastoral rounds to talk to an old ploughman in the country. Although his words were often unrefined, Spurgeon found that he often spoke great wisdom.

In one conversation, the man said to Spurgeon: "The other day, sir, the devil was tempting me and I tried to answer him; but I found he was an old lawyer and understood the law a great deal better than I did, so I gave over and would not argue with him anymore."

"What was he tempting you about?" Spurgeon asked.

"I asked him, 'What do you trouble me for?'

"'Why,' said he, 'about your soul.'

"'Oh!' said I, 'that is no business of mine. I have given my soul over into the hand of Christ. I have transferred everything to Him. If you want an answer to your doubts and queries, you must apply to my Advocate.'"

Two of the enemy's foremost temptations are these: the temptation to worry about what might happen as a consequence of our past sin, and the temptation to believe that we have not been forgiven by God. These worries can be resolved quickly by pointing the devil to the Cross. Our lives and eternal souls are in the hands that were nailed to it.

Thankfulness

In everything give thanks; for this is the will of God in Christ Jesus for you.

1 Thessalonians 5:18 NKJV

Give thanks to the LORD, for he is good; his love endures forever.

Psalm 107:1

You have turned my mourning into joyful dancing. You have taken away my clothes of mourning and clothed me with joy, that I might sing praises to you and not be silent. O LORD my God, I will give you thanks forever!

Psalm 30:11-12 NLT

O come, let us sing for joy to the LORD; let us shout joyfully to the rock of our salvation. Let us come before His presence with thanksgiving.

Psalm 95:1-2 NASB

It's All About Relationship

Imagine for a moment that someone you love comes to you and asks to borrow a small sum of money. You no doubt would lend it gladly, in part because of the close relationship you share.

Now imagine that this same person continues to come to you, asking for loans, food, clothing, the use of your car, a place to stay, and to borrow tools and appliances. While you do love this person, you would probably begin to feel that something was wrong. It's not the asking, but the attitude.

What causes the dilemma in this type of situation? The person who is coming with requests no longer sees his friend as someone with thoughts and feelings, but as a source of goods and services. So often we come to God in prayer with our request list in hand—"God, please do this . . ." or "God, I want . . ." We are wise to reconsider our relationship with God in prayer. Who is this One to Whom we pray? How good has He been to us? Doesn't He deserve our praise and thanksgiving?

We are missing out on the incredible benefits of an intimate relationship with God when we always come to Him with an empty hand, instead of a heart full of praise and thanksgiving.

Thankfulness

Let your conversation be without covetousness; and be content with such things as ye have: for he hath said, I will never leave thee, nor forsake thee.
Hebrews 13:5 KJV

I have learned in whatever state I am, to be content: I know how to be abased, and I know how to abound. Everywhere and in all things I have learned both to be full and to be hungry, both to abound and to suffer need. I can do all things through Christ who strengthens me.
Philippians 4:11-13 NKJV

And we know that God causes all things to work together for good to those who love God, to those who are called according to His purpose.
Romans 8:28 NASB

He who dwells in the shelter of the Most High will rest in the shadow of the Almighty.
Psalm 91:1

Thankfully Content

In *Little Women,* Mrs. March tells this story to her daughters:

"Once upon a time, there were four girls, who had enough to eat and drink and wear, a good many comforts and pleasures . . . and yet they were not contented. . . . These girls . . . made many excellent resolutions; but they . . . were constantly saying, 'If we only had this,' or 'If we could only do that.' . . . So they asked an old woman what spell they could use to make them happy, and she said, 'When you feel discontented, think over your blessings, and be grateful.'

"They decided to try her advice, and soon were surprised to see how well off they were. One discovered that money couldn't keep shame and sorrow out of rich people's houses; another that . . . she was a great deal happier with her youth, health, and good spirits than a certain fretful, feeble old lady, who couldn't enjoy her comforts; a third that, disagreeable as it was to help get dinner, it was harder still to have to go begging for it; and the fourth, that even carnelian rings were not so valuable as good behavior."

Remember that discontentment is rooted in ungratefulness. Teach your children the secret of contentment by teaching them to be thankful.

Tragedy

He heals the brokenhearted and binds up their wounds.

Psalm 147:3

Arise, shine; for your light has come, and the glory of the LORD has risen upon you. For behold, darkness will cover the earth, and deep darkness the peoples; but the LORD will rise upon you, And His glory will appear upon you.

Isaiah 60:1-2 NASB

For You have been a defense for the helpless, a defense for the needy in his distress, a refuge from the storm, a shade from the heat.

Isaiah 25:4 NASB

For I am convinced that nothing can ever separate us from his love. Death can't, and life can't. The angels won't, and all the powers of hell itself cannot keep God's love away. Our fears for today, our worries about tomorrow, or where we are— high above the sky, or in the deepest ocean— nothing will ever be able to separate us from the love of God demonstrated by our Lord Jesus Christ when he died for us.

Romans 8:38-39 TLB

Paths of Mercy and Truth

Beverly Sills has thrilled audiences with her beautiful operatic voice for years. Few people know, however, that her natural daughter was born deaf and that she has a stepdaughter who is also severely handicapped.

She writes in her autobiography, *Bubbles:*

"I was now only thirty-four, but a very mature thirty-four. In a strange way my children had brought me an inner peace. The first question I had when I learned of their tragedies was self-pitying, 'Why me?' Then gradually it changed to a much more important, 'Why them?' Despite their handicaps they were showing enormous strength in continuing to live as normal and constructive lives as possible. How could Peter and I show any less strength?"

Oscar Wilde once wrote: "In this world there are only two tragedies. One is not getting what one wants, and the other is getting it." A third tragedy may be added: the tragedy of not being able to go forward after tragedy has occurred. When a tragedy strikes, our first tendency is to ask "Why?" We may never know "why," but God promises to be with us always. When we make the decision to go on with life, He leads us on in His paths of mercy and truth.

Tragedy

The eternal God is a dwelling place, and underneath are the everlasting arms; and He drove out the enemy from before you, and said, "Destroy!"

Deuteronomy 33:27 NASB

Even when walking through the dark valley of death I will not be afraid, for you are close beside me, guarding, guiding all the way.

Psalm 23:4 TLB

When you pass through the waters, I will be with you; and when you pass through the rivers, they will not sweep over you. When you walk through the fire, you will not be burned; the flames will not set you ablaze.

Isaiah 43:2

I have told you these things, so that in me you may have peace. In this world you will have trouble. But take heart! I have overcome the world.

John 16:33

Deep Roots

Many people see abundant spring rains as a great blessing to farmers, especially if the rains come after the plants have sprouted and are several inches tall. What they don't realize is that even a short drought can have a devastating effect on a crop of seedlings that has received too much rain.

Why? Because during frequent rains, the young plants are not required to push their roots deeper into the soil in search of water. If a drought occurs later, plants with shallow root systems will quickly die.

We often receive abundance in our lives— rich fellowship, great teaching, thorough "soakings" of spiritual blessings. Yet when stress or tragedy enters our lives, we may find ourselves thinking God has abandoned us or is unfaithful. The fact is, we have allowed the "easiness" of our lives to keep us from pushing our spiritual roots deeper. We have allowed others to spoon-feed us, rather than develop our own deep personal relationship with God through prayer and study of His Word.

Only the deeply rooted are able to endure hard times without wilting. The best advice is to enjoy the "rain" while seeking to grow even closer to Him.

Wisdom

I will praise the LORD, who counsels me; even at night my heart instructs me.

Psalm 16:7

The LORD grants wisdom! From his mouth come knowledge and understanding.

Proverbs 2:6 NLT

For the foolishness of God is wiser than men, and the weakness of God is stronger than men.

1 Corinthians 1:25 RSV

God has chosen the foolish things of the world to shame the wise, and God has chosen the weak things of the world to shame the things which are strong.

1 Corinthians 1:27 NASB

Life Buoys

Sara Orne Jewett has written a beautiful novel about Maine, *The Country of the Pointed Firs*. In it, she describes the path that leads a woman writer from her home to that of a retired sea captain named Elijah Tilley. On the way, there are a number of wooden stakes in the ground that appear to be randomly scattered on his property. Each is painted white and trimmed in yellow, just like the captain's house.

Once she arrives at the captain's abode, the writer asks Captain Tilley what the stakes mean. He tells her that when he first made the transition from sailing the seas to plowing the land, he discovered his plow would catch on many of the large rocks just beneath the surface of the ground. Recalling how buoys in the sea always marked trouble spots for him, he set out the stakes as "land buoys" to mark the rocks. Then he could avoid plowing over them in the future.

God's promises and commandments are like buoys for us, revealing the trouble spots and rocky points of life. When we follow the wisdom found in God's Word and thereby steer clear of what is harmful to us, life is not only more enjoyable, but more productive.

Wisdom

If you want to know what God wants you to do, ask him, and he will gladly tell you, for he is always ready to give a bountiful supply of wisdom to all who ask him; he will not resent it.

James 1:5 TLB

Praise be to the name of God for ever and ever; wisdom and power are his. He reveals deep and hidden things; he knows what lies in darkness, and light dwells with him.

Daniel 2:20,22

In whom are hid all the treasures of wisdom and knowledge.

Colossians 2:3 KJV

The LORD by wisdom founded the earth; by understanding He established the heavens.

Proverbs 3:19 NKJV

The Beginning of Wisdom

A longing for God's wisdom must always be coupled
with reverence and understanding for justice, as this
statement from the St. Hilda Community attests:

As one who travels in the heat longs for cool waters,
So do I yearn for wisdom;
And as one who is weary with walking, so shall I sit
At her well and drink.

For her words are like streams in the desert; she is
like rain on parched ground, like a fountain whose
waters fail not.
Whoever hears her voice will be content with
nothing less; and whoever drinks of her will long
for more.

But who can find wisdom's dwelling place, and
who has searched her out?
For many have said to me, lo, here is wisdom, and
there you shall find understanding; here is true
worship of God, and thus shall your soul be satisfied.

But there was no delight in my soul; all my senses
were held in check.
My body became alien to me, and my heart was
shriveled within me.
For I sought understanding without justice; discern-
ment without the fear of God.

Worship

Therefore, I urge you, brothers, in view of God's mercy, to offer your bodies as living sacrifices, holy and pleasing to God—this is your spiritual act of worship.

Romans 12:1

For God bought you with a high price. So you must honor God with your body.

1 Corinthians 6:20 NLT

Spread for me a banquet of praise, serve High God a feast of kept promises.

Psalm 50:15 THE MESSAGE

I will praise you, O Lord my God, with all my heart; I will glorify your name forever.

Psalm 86:12

Autumn Dance

In *Mothering by Heart*, Robin Jones Gunn writes of this example of unashamed worship of our Creator:

"She stood a short distance from her guardian at the park this afternoon, her distinctive features revealing that although her body blossomed into young adulthood, her mind would always remain a child's. My children ran and jumped and sifted sand through perfect, coordinated fingers. Caught up in fighting over a shovel, they didn't notice when the wind changed. But she did. A wild autumn wind spinning leaves into amber flurries.

"I called to my boisterous son and jostled my daughter. Time to go. . . . My rosy-cheeked boy stood tall, watching with wide-eyed fascination the gyrating dance of the Down's syndrome girl as she scooped up leaves and showered herself with a twirling rain of autumn jubilation.

"With each twist and hop she sang deep, earthy grunts—a canticle of praise meant only for the One whose breath causes the leaves to tremble from the trees.

"Hurry up. Let's go. Seat belts on? I start the car. In the rearview mirror I study her one more time through misty eyes. And then the tears come. Not tears of pity for her. The tears are for me. For I am far too sophisticated to publicly shout praises to my Creator."

Worship

Let your good deeds shine out for all to see, so that everyone will praise your heavenly Father.
Matthew 5:16 NLT

Whatever you do, work at it with all your heart, as working for the Lord, not for men.
Colossians 3:23

And whatever you do or say, let it be as a representative of the Lord Jesus, all the while giving thanks through him to God the Father.
Colossians 3:17 NLT

Shout Hallelujah, you God-worshipers; give glory, you sons of Jacob; adore him, you daughters of Israel. He has never let you down, never looked the other way when you were being kicked around.
Psalm 22:23-24 THE MESSAGE

Worship and Worry

Ruth Bell Graham tells the story of when God taught her that worship is the antidote for worry. She was in a foreign country, wide-awake at 3 a.m. So she began to pray for one who was running away from God. She says, "When it is dark and the imagination runs wild, there are fears only a mother can understand."

Then suddenly, the Lord told her to "quit studying the problem and start studying the promises." So she opened her Bible and began to read Philippians 4:6 KJV: "Be careful for nothing; but in everything by prayer and supplication *with thanksgiving. . . .*"

"Suddenly I realized the missing ingredient in my prayers had been 'with thanksgiving.' So I put down my Bible and spent time worshipping Him for Who and What He is. This covers more territory than any one mortal can comprehend. Even contemplating what little we do know dissolves doubts, reinforces faith, and restores joy.

"It was as if someone turned on the lights in my mind and heart, and the little fears and worries that had been nibbling away in the darkness like mice and cockroaches hurriedly scuttled for cover.

"That was when I learned that worship and worry cannot live in the same heart: they are mutually exclusive."

Additional copies of this book and other titles from
Honor Books are available from your local bookstore:

God's Little Lessons on Life
God's Little Lessons on Life for Dad
God's Little Lessons on Life for Mom
God's Little Lessons on Life for Graduates

If you have enjoyed this book, or if it has impacted
your life, we would like to hear from you.

Please contact us at:

Honor Books
Department E
P. O. Box 55388
Tulsa, Oklahoma 74137
Or by email at info@honorbooks.com